I0200326

Happiness Is You

BY MAKING A HABIT OF HAPPINESS, YOU CAN EXPERIENCE BLISS IN YOUR DAILY LIFE

By

DR. SIDDHARTHA B. GAUTAM

Copyright © 2012 Dr. Siddhartha B. Gautam

All rights reserved.

ISBN: 0615633439

ISBN 13:   9780615633435

Library of Congress Control Number: LCCN: 2012938320

Step Press

Fayetteville, NC

CreateSpace, North Charleston, SC

DEDICATION

This book is dedicated to my parents whose life was a living example of happiness and simplicity. As a first-hand witness to the genuine embodiment of happiness in their day-to-day existence, I remain eternally grateful to them for having imparted these important life skills to me.

Table of Contents

I

Happiness Is You

A journey of a thousand miles begins with a single step.

— LAO-TZU

---

have often used this quotation in my motivational talks around the country, and this is the way you hear the words of this Chinese philosopher quoted most often. But I have also seen it translated from the original Chinese this way: "The journey of a thousand miles begins beneath your feet." That subtle difference is the way I want to begin this book.

There are so many books about happiness on the market right now. When I first began to write this book, I did a quick search and found more than 2,800 nonfiction books with the word *happiness* in the title, with a dozen of those published in the previous thirty days. Those numbers tell me at least two things: first, that millions of readers are searching for happiness, and second, that they are not finding it. Otherwise, why would books on the topic continue to be published?

I too was once one of those seekers. Many years ago I came from my native India to America, the land of opportunity, where the roads are paved with gold. I devoted myself to the pursuit of the American dream, getting up at four o'clock in the morning and working till nine o'clock at night, building up my consulting practice. With hard work I achieved the dream: a house, two cars, and plenty of possessions to keep up with the Joneses.

I had achieved everything, but somehow I had lost what my father back in India—who had never owned more than two pieces of clothing in his life—had always possessed: happiness.

I began to realize this when I went back to India on a visit. When I first left for America, I had promised my father I would return home when I had saved ten thousand dollars. So he asked me if I had saved that much money yet. I had, but now I didn't think that would be enough to sustain the lifestyle I had so quickly become accustomed to. I told my father, "When I have one hundred thousand, I'll come back."

My father shook his head sadly. "Son, you will never have enough savings and you will never come back." He could not understand why anyone with a vast fortune of ten thousand American dollars could possibly have need for more. "Why are you worried?" he asked, in his simple, straightforward way.

His question continued to haunt me after I returned to America. Why was I worried? I had more than enough to meet my needs. I had a loving wife and family. I had the respect and admiration of my colleagues and clients. Why was I so restless? Why was happiness so elusive?

One day I came across the answer in a twenty-two-page pamphlet by Swami Dayananda, printed in large letters on the plain, unadorned cover: "The Problem is You. The Solution is You." Suddenly I realized that I was trying to find something outside, in the world, that truly only exists within, in myself. The swami's words were uplifting and discouraging at the same time. Now I knew where true happiness could be found, and it was not on some remote mountaintop or at the bottom of the sea. It was within me. I was the answer to my quest. But if happiness was really so close, why wasn't I experiencing it? Because I was also the problem. I myself was the obstacle that separated me from bliss.

Is it hard to understand how something can be both the problem and the solution? The swami illustrated what he meant with a story about a man who sat down to read the newspaper one morning but couldn't find his reading glasses. He searched the drawers of his desk, all over the table, even on the floor. "Where are my glasses?" he shouted so loudly that his whole family came running to help. Finally his youngest son pointed to the glasses, which were sitting on top of the man's head. He'd had them all along. He had been searching high and low for something that he possessed the whole time. He was the problem and he was the solution. But—and here's a key point for relentless seekers of happiness—the reason he was the problem was that he didn't *know* he was the solution. He was ignorant of what he had readily within his grasp.

When we seek our happiness outside ourselves—by acquiring more possessions, by pursuing a better job, by accumulating more money—we are like the man fruitlessly searching for his glasses. Just as he convinced himself that his glasses were hopelessly lost, we can convince ourselves that we are unhappy. That is the power the mind holds over us.

Yet the mind can also work to our advantage. We have all experienced moments when everything seems to be going wrong: You miss the bus. It starts to rain. A truck comes by and splashes the water from a puddle all over your clothes. Your umbrella breaks. You arrive at work an hour late—wet, dirty, and mad—only to realize it's a Saturday and you didn't need to come in at all. How do you react? Do you scream and rant? Do you break down in tears? Or do you have a good laugh at yourself? Look carefully at the situation. The facts are the same: you are wet and dirty, with a broken umbrella and spoiled clothes. But your *response* to the situation determines how you feel about it. You control whether you are happy or unhappy.

As the swami says, "All that is required to be free from sadness is that you look at yourself as you are." The more I thought about that statement, the easier it became to understand what had been so mystifying before. My father was content with his two pieces of clothing because he knew who he was and where his true happiness dwelt. Yet I knew very successful businessmen who were never content with their big houses, fancy cars, and many possessions because they were too busy pursuing happiness to ever truly experience it. I realized I was one of those people. I was the problem.

But the good news was that I was also the solution. Now that I knew where true happiness could be found, the challenge became removing the impediments in my life that separated me from it. It was the difference between following a map to find buried treasure and actually doing the digging to get to the treasure. The task was simple but not easy. I began to dig.

I started to look at myself as I am, to strip away all of those trappings that I thought defined me. I was not the house or even the neighborhood I lived in. If I bought a different house or moved to a different city, I was still myself. I was not the car I drove. I had owned many different cars and none of them had ever changed who I was. In fact, none of my possessions had influenced my basic personality. A new gadget might make my life easier or a new suit might lift my spirits, but I was still the same person on the inside.

Think about that for a moment. How much of your own unhappiness is rooted in this common misunderstanding of self? It's not surprising how often we fall prey to this faulty reasoning, especially since the whole industry of retail sales is devoted to it. The underlying message is that if you just buy this particular item, it will make you happier. But then, of course, it doesn't, so then you have to buy something else, something newer, brighter, shinier. The manufacturers and salespeople and advertisers of the world have convinced many of us that material items will make us happy.

I dug deeper. I realized that I was not the job I held. If I got fired today, I wouldn't cease to exist. Neither was I the titles or the degrees I had earned. These concepts may be harder for you to accept. Most people don't really think that they are what they own, when they stop long enough to consider it. But we feel different about our work. We often introduce ourselves to others by our job titles: I am an accountant. I am a doctor. I work with children. Yet, as so many people discover during periods of recession, your work does not define you. While there are sad stories that come as a result of layoffs and forced retirements, many people use an unplanned change in circumstances to their advantage. Some start new careers, find fulfillment in volunteer work, or rekindle former interests. These are the people who know that they are more than a job title and know where their true happiness lies.

Now I was getting closer to what I really was. I was definitely not my money or possessions, nor my job or education. But surely part of my essential being must be the people in my life. My identity must be wrapped up in my roles as husband, father, friend. But the deeper I dug, I realized that as much as I love my dear wife, family, and friends, even they are not what defines me. If something were to happen to them, I would grieve, as I did for my parents, but I would still be the same person.

Does this sound heartless? Try looking at it this way: Think of someone you know who has been what we call "unlucky in love." They are always looking for that one special person who will make them happy, yet they never find him or her. That's because no other person can ever make us happy, no matter how much she loves us or we love her. We either are happy or we aren't, based on who we are.

So now I dug down even deeper: Who am I? The more I meditated on that question, the better I understood that I was not even the body I inhabit. This face I see in the mirror each morning, these legs I walk with every day, this stomach I feed at every meal, this heart that beats within me more than 100,000 times a day — none of them is actually me.

Remember how I compared this inward journey to digging for a treasure chest? No one digging for treasure stops when he or she reaches the chest and says, "Oh, what a nice, sturdy chest. I'm so happy I found it." No, everyone knows that the true treasure lies within the chest. The same is true of your body. It is only the container for your true self; it isn't your real identity. It can be nicked and scarred or buffed and polished to a high shine. It doesn't matter which — neither affects the treasure within.

You can also think of your body as a vehicle for your true self. Just as you drive around in your car and keep it (I hope) properly maintained, you also take care of your body as it gets you from place to place. But you are no more your body than you are your car.

So if we are not our possessions or our relationships or even our body, then who are we? Here is what is so exciting: We are no less than that endless reservoir of bliss that we seek. We are all divine creatures living a human experience, inhabiting a human body. But it is that divinity within that is the source of the reservoir.

Now it took me years to get to this realization, and I still stumble on occasion. I come to you as a fellow sufferer; every bad habit I talk about, I have done. I was the sinner who did all these things. I am not holier than thou. But I have changed my approach to life, and I want to share with you the tools I used to do it. If I can change, you can too. No special, secret formula exists. Everyone can achieve this state. All you really need is an intensity of desire and a daily commitment. You can go at your own pace, and it is never too late to start. Self-discovery is better late than never.

The reason I believe you can find this reservoir of bliss is that I know it exists within you, as surely as it exists within me. No matter what we look like on the outside, we share a common divinity inside. Removing the impediments that keep us from experiencing that divinity is what enables us to understand ourselves and to understand others. (Let me be clear: When I say "divinity," I am not referring to any religion in particular. As Mohandas Gandhi wrote in his final days, "It is no consequence by what name we call God in our homes.")

If it's hard to grasp the idea of a common divinity, think of it as a fire. When a bonfire blazes, it throws off sparks. Sparks are smaller, but each has all the properties of that original fire, its source. Each of us is a spark. Often we forget what we came from, our origin. Often we don't recognize that the spark within us is part of that larger fire—and we don't see the same spark that exists within others.

Right now you may be thinking, "But this is all too simple. Happiness can't really be that easy." It is simple, but not easy. I may not be telling you anything you haven't read or heard before about happiness. But the key, and why you are still searching, is that you haven't learned to apply what you know in your everyday life.

Let me give you an example. When I was chairman of the board at our local hospital, we had a problem with patients catching infections and viruses because not all the doctors washed their hands between patients. The germs from one patient were being passed along to another by the doctor. So we put up signs and gave incentives to the doctors to make sure they remembered to wash their hands between patients. The infection rate in the patients went down significantly.

Having gone through this process, I had no doubt in my mind that washing hands prevents infections. I knew it was a fact. Yet a few weeks later, I caught a cold, probably because I didn't always wash my hands before eating. I knew what I should be doing, but I failed to do it. From then on, I tried to make it a habit to wash my hands always before sitting down to a meal. My wife would remind me to wash up in the kitchen each time, even if I had just washed my hands in the bathroom. It seemed unnecessary, but it reinforced the idea of hand-washing before eating by associating the habit with the kitchen. Now it's a habit that I don't even need to think about anymore, and I haven't had a cold in two years.

In my case and at the hospital, such simple advice had a tremendous impact on health. Washing your hands is a simple task, but remembering to do it each time you should isn't easy. And you won't get the results you want if you do it only once. You have to make it a habit.

How do you make happiness a habit? That is what I hope to discuss in this book. And just as I learned to incorporate hand-washing into my daily routine, I want to show you how you can incorporate happiness into the life you are living now. I am not going to tell you to become a hermit or spend all day in silent meditation or even take a pilgrimage or go on a retreat. Since you are the solution to your problem, it doesn't matter where you start your journey.

This is not a recipe book for happiness, nor is it a step-by-step guide. You already have happiness within you. As I say, happiness *is* you. So what I want to help you do is to remove the impediments that keep you from experiencing that happiness in your life every day. Actually, what will be more important than what you learn will be what you "unlearn" as part of this process. Through silence, meditation, yoga, and what I call the "magic and mystery of simplicity," you will gradually strip away all of life's distractions and experience the bliss in the core of your being.

Each chapter that follows will address impediments that keep us from experiencing the happiness within us — greed, desires, frustrations — and qualities we need to develop to enrich our lives — compassion, generosity, simplicity. Each chapter will also include questions to ask yourself that will help you to gauge your own progress and a reminder to do a specific action that will help you make happiness a habit. In addition, I will provide a general, daily to-do list at the end of the book incorporating the principles discussed throughout the book. Just as a pilot reviews a checklist before and after each flight, you should check this list each morning as a reminder of what you should be doing every day and review it each evening to check your progress. Each day you make happiness a habit, you are one step closer to that endless reservoir of bliss within us all.

At the same time, you will be discovering who you are and how to be contented and confident. This self-awareness is not to be confused with ego. Ego makes demands upon others: Listen to me! Show me respect! Do what I say! We may think of the egotistical person as one who looks down on others, but in reality, the egoist is begging for the attention, respect, and agreement of other people. Only then can the egoist be happy.

But the truly happy person doesn't rely on others to feel better. These are the people who don't need to put up a false front to try to impress or intimidate you. With them, what you see is what you get. And, while they generally like other people, they are also comfortable all by themselves, even for long stretches at a time. When you are in the presence of such people, you can feel the serenity and tranquility emanating from them.

One such person was a widely respected swami who came out into the wider world so seldom that he was not familiar with the practice of being put on hold when making a telephone call. He turned to his companions with a questioning look when the music began to play.

"They play the music so you won't get lonely," one of the others explained.

The swami laughed. "Do they really think I will get lonely if there is no one else to talk to? Do they not realize that you can be alone without being lonely?"

Sadly, most of us don't have that realization. We avoid being alone at any cost. Often, those lacking human companionship turn to animals for warmth and affection. Various scientific studies confirm that proximity to pets is healing and raises the level of the feel-good neuro-chemical oxytocin in the brain. But Americans had sixty-one million pets in 1991; today we have 161 million animal companions. Why has there been such a dramatic increase in the number of pets, and why do we spend so much (an estimated $48 billion each year) on their care? Certainly not everyone gets a pet as insurance against loneliness, but the numbers seem to show that making a pet part of their lives is one way Americans avoid being alone.

Why are we so afraid of being alone? Part of the reason is that being alone forces you to face who you are and most of us strive to avoid that kind of self-awareness. But this is precisely what you need to do in order to experience happiness. Look at yourself as you are, a spiritual being having a human experience, a being full of faults and virtues. Now accept that person and get to know that person better. Love that person, because you will never truly be able to love others if you don't also love yourself—again, not in an egotistical way, but in a healthy, accepting way.

There is no better time to start than today. The journey begins beneath your feet. Happiness is you.

Checklist:

At the end of each chapter, I will ask you to take a few minutes to determine where you are on a "happiness scale." You can rate yourself on a scale of one to ten, with one being miserable or depressed and ten being blissful or ecstatic. If it helps, you can refer to this visual cue as a guide:

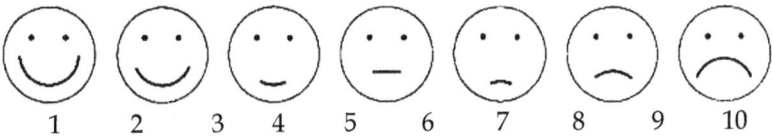

The Faces Scale (Andrews & Withey, 1976)

Record your rating in a way that works for you—in a daily journal or diary, in a computer log, in your smartphone—along with a few notes about what most affected your mood today. Was it rainy or sunny? Did you have a fight with anyone? Did someone do you a favor? Just jot down what comes to mind quickly and review later on to see if you detect any patterns. This is part of the process of self-awareness.

I will also give you an exercise to do or a list of questions to meditate upon related to the chapter you have just read. For this chapter, here is an exercise to help you think about the difference between the person you appear to be and the person you really are. It works better for those who are already age seventy or so, but anyone can benefit from it: Write your own eulogy. Make it an honest appraisal of who you are, what is important to you, and what you hope to leave behind as your impact on others. When you have finished, close the door and read it aloud to yourself alone.

Now meditate for a while on these questions:

- Are you happy with what can be said about the life you have lived?

- If you aren't, what would you change?

- What would you like to include in your eulogy?

- How do you want to be remembered?

It's not too late for a rewrite. Write a eulogy for the person you want to be and then let yourself become that person. That is who you truly are. Let the world see that person.

Reminder for today:

Today I will spend time alone without feeling lonely.

2

True Happiness Is the Goal

Oh, how bitter a thing it is to look into happiness through another man's eyes.

— WILLIAM SHAKESPEARE, AS YOU LIKE IT

What is it that makes you happy? For King Midas, in the fable told by the ancient Greeks, it was gold. He loved everything about it— the glitter, the shine, the weight, the color. To Midas, anything that wasn't golden was a disappointment. He wished everything could be made of gold. So when the god Dionysius, in gratitude for the king's hospitality, granted him one wish, Midas wished that everything he touched would turn to gold. Dionysius warned the king that his wish might have unintended consequences, but Midas was too excited to care. He ran from room to room in his palace, touching all his possessions and watching as they turned into gold. Simple wooden chairs became stately golden ones. Plain pottery plates transformed into priceless dinnerware. From floor to ceiling, from the throne room to his beloved rose garden, the king gave everything the same golden glow.

Feeling very pleased with his morning's work, King Midas sat down to breakfast. But every time he reached for a juicy orange or a tender piece of bread, it too turned into glittering gold. The king was accumulating wealth very quickly, but growing hungrier by the minute. He decided he might as well go back to bed, but the minute his head touched the pillow, it turned from downy softness to hard, cold metal.

Just as he was beginning to realize the wisdom of Dionysius's warning about the golden touch, his little daughter rushed into his room in tears, holding in her hands one of the new brittle flowers that no longer had a rose's sweet perfume. Midas took the girl in his arms to comfort her, but turned her into a golden statue instead. The distraught king begged the god to be rid of what he now thought of as a curse instead of a gift, forever cured of his greed for gold.

While I hope none of you would be so foolish as to wish for the Golden Touch, sometimes we do act very much like King Midas, becoming so consumed by the pursuit of wealth that we forget what is important in life, what brings us true happiness. So before we begin this inward journey that I described in the previous chapter, let us pause for a moment to talk about our goal. What do I mean by true happiness?

Like King Midas, many people (and I once was one of them) confuse happiness with wealth. But happiness is not something you can measure in terms of money. The

Beatles told us years ago that money can't buy you love. It also can't buy you happiness.

Citing lectures by British economist Lord Richard Layard, an article in the *Guardian* at the height of the economic boom at the turn of this century declared, "Happiness has not risen in western nations in the last fifty years despite massive increases in wealth."

Interestingly, researchers reached the same conclusion after the economic downturn. In 2010, Gallup released its first worldwide poll on happiness and money. More than 136,000 people from 132 countries answered questions about their income and their attitudes. The survey found that while it was true that life satisfaction generally rose with income, the enjoyment of life or day-to-day happiness did not. That is, people who made more money *thought* they were better off but they didn't really *feel* happier because of their income.

In fact, Layard reasoned, wealth can even be the cause of great misery, when a person compares his income and possessions with another person's. You may be happy with your new Chevy sedan, until your neighbor gets a new Porsche. Suddenly your car seems slow and old-fashioned. It's exactly the same car, but your attitude about it has changed because you are jealous of your neighbor. You are determined to get a car that is just as fast and powerful as your neighbor's, no matter what the cost. So you either go into debt with an expensive loan, or you spend many extra hours working and miss out on other activities, time with your family, or just relaxing.

Perhaps you don't care so much about money or material possessions, but you do like to pursue other pleasures. You indulge in too much food, too much wine, too many romantic partners, always searching for a new rush of excitement. But as with possessions, the pleasure these indulgences bring is only temporary, and each pursuit requires more effort to produce the desired effect.

This never-ending pursuit has been called the "hedonic treadmill." You race and race just to stay even, never getting ahead, never reaching your goal. You chase happiness as it flits and floats on gossamer wings, tantalizing you with its beauty. You always think that you see it just ahead of you, yet you are never able to reach it. It always eludes your grasp. I confess that I spent much of my own life on that hedonic treadmill. For the first fifty years of my life, everything was important—or at least that's what I believed—and just out of my reach.

Why can you never reach the goal of happiness in this pursuit? Because it is a system designed to fail. Whenever you believe that a material object or even another person—anything or anyone that you desire—has the power to make you happy, you are doomed to be disappointed. If your thoughts are ruled by your desires, you just increase your levels of stress and unhappiness each time those desires go unmet.

Even if you succeed in your pursuit, you will not be content. I am sure you have run into this situation in your own life. Think back to a time when you finally achieved that dream job, that dream vacation, that dream home. How did you feel? Were you elated at your achievement? Or did you feel a letdown instead, now that the pursuit was done?

Maybe you don't think of yourself as particularly hedonistic. You don't feel as though you are a slave to advertising, the prevailing consumer culture, or the pursuit of pleasures. But you do have unmet desires that make you feel restless, discontented, like something in your life is missing, even if you can't express exactly what it is. These unarticulated desires also come between you and happiness.

Recently I contracted pneumonia and spent time in a hospital for the first time in my life. While I was there under doctor's orders to rest, I began to think about how desires are like viruses. They attack and grow inside us, spreading throughout our body, spreading to other people, making us weaker each day, leaving us more vulnerable to the next infection that comes our way.

These viruses of desire set us up for unhappiness. In the hospital, I pondered what Vedic scriptures (the spiritual literature of the ancient Indian culture) call the enemies of happiness: pleasure-seeking, anger, greed, delusion, pride, and jealousy. I was amazed at how most of these enemies are rooted in an inappropriate desire. If we can only learn to minimize or eliminate these desires, we can defeat the enemies of happiness.

Worry and discontent also come between us and happiness. Worrying is like rocking in a rocking chair; it keeps you busy and in constant motion, but you never get anywhere. Likewise with discontent, which Swami Sukhbodhananda described in his book, *Oh, Mind, Relax, Please!*, as a crack in a pot: "Water poured into a cracked pot will not remain in it. Similarly, people without contentment cannot be happy. They will only worry about what they do not possess. Their hearts are always full of sorrow. Once the crack in the pot is sealed, it would hold water poured into it. Similarly, when the blind spots of the mind are removed, it would be filled with joy."

In his book *The Total Money Makeover: A Proven Plan for Financial Fitness*, financial writer and radio show host David Ramsey described the futility of the hedonic wheel this way: "We buy things we don't need with money we don't have to impress people we don't like." Do you see how this kind of thinking is really letting other people dictate to you what should make you happy? Other people, often people you don't even know, are setting your expectations for happiness. As a close friend observed, "You are the CEO of your own happiness." As the CEO, you get to decide your mindset.

We spend so much time, effort, and money on the pursuit of happiness. Not only do we chase after happiness with credit card in hand, we also go to special seminars and retreats and read books about how other people found their bliss, hoping we can follow in their footsteps. But how useful is this? Most of us just cannot afford to drop everything to travel the world seeking happiness.

What makes this fruitless pursuit so ironic is that we don't need to go anywhere or buy anything to find the source of true happiness. The source of true contentment is not external. You can only find happiness by taking an inward journey.

More than a century ago, the great American essayist Ralph Waldo Emerson wrote, "Nothing can bring you happiness but yourself," and it's still true today. Happiness is not only *within* you. Happiness *is* you.

But you are saying, "How can you say happiness is me when I don't feel happy? If happiness was inside me, wouldn't I know it? Wouldn't I feel it?"

Those are good questions. There is a story of a yogi who played a trick on a rich man to show him where happiness lies. The rich man was very sad and came to the yogi to give up his wealth and seek true happiness. But the yogi snatched the bag of treasure and ran away with it. The rich man chased after him until they both came back to where they had started. The yogi handed the money back to the man with a smile. "All this wealth was with you even before you came here. But you did not derive joy from it," the yogi explained. "It is the same wealth that is with you now, but you have found a great joy in your heart! So where did the happiness come from—from wealth or from within you?"

Let me ask you a similar question: What are the moments in your life when you have felt the happiest, the most content, the most at peace? I'm willing to bet that they weren't when you were consciously seeking pleasure. Instead, your special moments are of loving touches, kind words, smiling children—the small gestures that bring great happiness.

You may not have realized it, but you have also glimpsed the source of this true happiness. Whenever you have felt a spontaneous urge to do a good deed or speak a gentle word or give a warm hug to someone in need, you experienced a rush of positive feelings, a gush of joy. Wouldn't you like to make that fleeting feeling stay? What if I said, through much practice and unlearning of your current habits, you could make that happiness your constant state?

Each of us has been endowed with an inexhaustible reservoir of happiness to discover and enjoy. By the time you finish this book, you will know once and for all that all of your happiness originates within you and how you can access that happiness on a daily basis.

To do this, you should be clear about what I mean by "happiness." I have told you what happiness is not. Now I will try to explain what it is. Happiness is nothing less than the state of bliss that is part of the divinity within us all. It is the contentment and peace that become ours when we embrace that divinity within ourselves and within others.

This is not to say that we are all gods, but rather—as expressed in various ways in the world's major religions—that we all share a divine presence within us. When Indians greet each other by saying, "Namaste," it literally means, "I bow to the God within you."

Acceptance of this attitude means there is no justification for treating people differently because of their sex, color, age, height, weight, or any other external characteristic. If we accept the same divinity within us all, then we must treat everyone with the same love and respect.

Although their scriptures express it differently, the world's major religions endorse the concept of the divinity within us. According to the Hindu's Vedic scriptures, we all are children of God, and have three main important characteristics of God: truth, consciousness, and bliss. The Jewish Torah teaches that people are made "in the image of God," and the Koran (50:16) colorfully quotes Allah as saying, "We are nearer to him (humankind) than the jugular vein."

In the Christian New Testament (Luke 17:21), Jesus expressed the thought of the divinity within even more clearly: "The kingdom of God is within you." That concept led Russian author Leo Tolstoy to write a book by that name to inspire people to live peacefully and to change their governments and cultures through nonviolent protests and demonstrations. One of the most enthusiastic readers of *The Kingdom of God Is Within You!* was the great Indian leader, Mahatma Mohandas Gandhi.

Gandhi had his own thoughts about happiness: "Happiness is when what you think, what you say, and what you do are in harmony." Think about that for a moment. Have you ever held your tongue and stood quietly by when you saw someone being unfairly treated? Have you ever just gone along with the crowd instead of speaking up for what you believe is right? How did that make you feel?

Now imagine feeling a quiet confidence within that gives you the strength to say and do what you know in your heart to be right. Imagine the positive energy that feeling would give you. Helping you achieve that harmony of thought, word, and deed is the purpose of this book.

Even economists and politicians are starting to realize that happiness has value. The British government has introduced a "happiness index" that will help shape policy in the future. Through surveys, researchers will gauge the population's feelings of general well-being and how they are faring in achieving their life goals. Similar ideas are being proposed in Canada and France as well. The hope is to be able to quantify a quality that has resisted being reduced to a statistical measure.

The Positive Psychology Institute, for example, uses an "authentic happiness inventory" to rate a person's contentment on a scale of one to five. A series of twenty-four multiple-choice questions lets you rate your feelings about work, success, your purpose in life, and how bored you get each day. (Hardly anyone scores a five, by the way. The average score is 3.2.)

Steve Forbes, publisher of *Forbes Magazine*, is famous for compiling the annual Forbes 500—the richest people in the world. But a friend of mine who heard him speak recently was surprised to hear him emphasize something other than wealth in his talk. "Life," Forbes told his audience, "is really about the pursuit of happiness." I wonder if that means we can soon expect a list of the world's happiest people in *Forbes Magazine*.

Achieving happiness is not easy, but it is not impossible. In life, all valuable and important things require hard work and persistence, and ultimately the result of your dedication and devotion is always sweeter. Just as you wouldn't expect to wake up one morning and say, "I think I'll run a marathon today" if you had never done any training, you should not expect to achieve lifelong bliss instantly after reading a few chapters of this book. The marathon runner starts with short distances and gradually increases his time and mileage. He focuses his mind on the task at hand, ignoring heat and cold, hunger, and pain. He prepares his body by eating certain foods and avoiding others.

In the same way, you will need to train your body, mind, and soul before you can hope to achieve lifelong bliss. You need to start slowly, maybe for as little as five minutes a day, but practice every day so that the training becomes a habit for you. For those five minutes, you will need to focus all your attention on your preparations. You cannot multitask, as you are expected to do in your work-day. You cannot be checking your phone or your e-mail because you're expected to be available 24/7. You will need to unplug yourself, literally and figuratively, from all those distractions that keep you from connecting to the happiness within you.

I will end this chapter with the story of a different king, this one in India long ago. This king was very depressed. His physicians couldn't find anything wrong with him physically, yet the king was wasting away before their eyes. Finally a visiting physician told the king that he knew how to solve his problem. Happiness was conta-gious, wasn't it? Don't you feel happier when other peo-ple around you are laughing and smiling? "So find the happiest man in your kingdom," he advised, "and bor-row his shirt and wear it, and that will make you happy too."

Right away, the king sent out a host of ministers to search the kingdom for the happiest man. But each time a minister approached a man, no matter how much he was laughing and enjoying himself, he would always say, "Oh, I'm not all that happy. Go to see my neighbor. He's the happiest man around." And so on. Finally, in despair, they returned to the palace dejected and told the king, "We can't find a happy man in the kingdom."

Meanwhile, the chief minister was still searching. Walking near a river one evening, he saw a man sitting quietly in the shadows and watching the water. "Are you happy?" the chief minister asked the man.

"Yes, I am," he answered.

So the chief minister explained his search and begged the man to help his king if he could. "Please let us borrow your shirt," he said.

But the man emerged from the shadows to reveal that he was not wearing a shirt, only a simple loincloth. "Tell your king that he doesn't need to borrow a shirt to find happiness," he told the chief minister. "Please tell the king that all happiness is inside."

Now you are clear about what your goal is and where you can find it. The rest of the book will be devoted to the journey. You will learn how to remove impediments to achieving true happiness and how to develop habits that will make happiness your normal state of being.

Checklist:

Take a few minutes to determine where you are on the happiness scale right now, on a scale of one to ten.

Now meditate for a while on these questions:

- What is it that makes you happy?

- What are the impediments to your happiness?

- What desires are hardest for you to control?

- If you were granted a wish like King Midas, what would you wish?

- What does your wish say about you?

Reminder for today:

Today I will pay attention to the little things in life that make me happy.

3

Silence Is Golden

Beware the barrenness of a busy life.

— SOCRATES

I n today's 24/7 world, we are proud to be busy. We keep ourselves plugged in wherever we go: taking our cell phones on vacation, checking our e-mail or our Facebook page constantly, staying in touch with world events as they happen by TV, radio, and Internet. Between work and family obligations, and with a variety of charitable, social, religious, and recreational activities crowded into our busy schedules, we are constantly on the go.

But, as Socrates observed, a full calendar doesn't mean a full life. When you live your life on the surface like that, time passes in a blur. One day you look in the mirror and see how much older you have become, yet you are no closer to achieving your life's goals. Worse, you find no joy in your daily life, and the never-ending routine of day-to-day living seems to have no point.

If you were living in a fable, this is the time when you would stop your daily routine and make a solitary journey to a remote location to find the meaning of life. I suppose fables are told this way because—difficult as it may be to leave friends and family—living the life of a monk or hermit is the surest way to achieve a high level of simplicity in life. But this is not a realistic solution in today's world. Even if you did go on a retreat, your boss would probably still expect you to check e-mail and your family would want to be able to reach you on your cell phone! With family, work, and community responsibilities, we aren't able to drop everything and join an ashram.

But you don't have to go away to experience happiness and contentment. Remember what I have been saying. Happiness is you. The problem is you. The solution is you. If the problem is you and the solution is you, then it doesn't matter where you are physically. You carry your happiness within you wherever you are. And unfortunately you can also carry around those impediments that keep you from experiencing that happiness. But you don't remove those impediments by escaping from them temporarily. You can start to strip away all of life's busy work and distractions right where you are. To reach that goal of true happiness, you need to simplify your life. You begin in a place of silence.

"There is no need to go to India or anywhere else to find peace," said Dr. Elisabeth Kubler-Ross, the psychiatrist best known for her explanation of the five stages of grief. "You will find that deep place of silence right in your room, your garden, or even your bathtub."

Dr. Kubler-Ross correctly makes the connection between the need for silence and finding inner peace. With so much competing for our attention, we literally cannot hear ourselves think. We need to turn down the volume in our lives.

But creating an atmosphere of silence is not easy in today's society. Music is piped into offices and elevators, and people with iPods carry their own soundtracks with them wherever they go. Thousands of TV and radio stations bombard us with news and entertainment around the clock, while the hum of machinery, the roar of traffic, and the constant drone of hundreds of voices, including our own, surround us with an atmosphere polluted by noise. Not only is this noise distracting, it's also unhealthy. Studies cited by the Environmental Protection Agency, which regulates noise pollution, show a direct link between noise and stress-related illnesses, high blood pressure, speech interference, hearing loss, sleep disruption, and lost productivity.

Even the farthest reaches of the deep blue sea are not immune to noise pollution. A new study published in *Scientific American* reveals that the sounds of offshore drilling, ship motors, sonar use, and pile driving are damaging whales, dolphins, squid, octopuses, and other ocean dwellers.

Yet excess noise is scarcely a new problem. Sir Richard Steele, who lived at the turn of the eighteenth century, wrote, "I have often lamented that we cannot close our ears with as much ease as we can our eyes." So much for simpler, quieter times.

Although we cannot close our ears to external noise, we are able to control our exposure to it, to an extent. Turn off the television, the radio, the CD and DVD players, the computer, even your telephone. It will seem strange at first because you are so accustomed to the buzz of constant noise. But soon you will appreciate the beauty and the joy that can be found in silence. "See how nature—trees, flowers, grass — grows in silence; see the stars, the moon, and the sun, how they move in silence," said Mother Teresa of Calcutta. "We need silence to be able to touch souls," including, I would add, your own.

But it will not be easy to silence yourself. We live in a society that puts a great emphasis on communication and talking. Silence is not something we welcome. Silence is even sometimes used as a punishment — teachers who sentence rowdy students to "silent lunch" or former friends who give us "the silent treatment."

We are suspicious of the silent. If a child is extremely quiet, we may think something is wrong, no matter what the other evidence. Albert Einstein's parents were concerned because their son was a late talker, not speaking until he was nearly three years old. According to a story told by Otto Neugebauer, a mathematician and historian of ancient mathematics, young Albert finally broke his silence at the supper table one night to say, "The soup is too hot." His parents, greatly relieved to hear their son's first words, asked him why he had never spoken before. "Because up to now everything was in order," young Albert replied.

I tell this story as a reminder that most of what we say isn't all that important. If we never told the world how we slept the night before or how expensive gasoline is getting or how well our children are doing in school, would it really matter? What if, like young Einstein, we held our tongues until there was something we needed to say?

Another important point about silence is that, when we choose to be silent, it is a sign of strength, not weakness. Think of American cowboy movies and the heroes known as "the strong, silent type." Or, more appropriately, think of the quiet dignity of those black Americans who showed the superiority of their character during the civil rights movement by *not* responding with harsh words when they were taunted and tortured by their tormentors. Their silence spoke volumes about their civility and strength and earned them the respect of reasonable people.

When I suggest that you should spend more time in silence, I'm not saying that you should go suddenly mute or never turn on your television again. Instead, you should develop a habit of silence. Start slowly, maybe as little as five minutes a day at the beginning, and gradually increase your silent time. For me, silence is easier in the morning than later in the day. When you wake up, don't automatically turn on the TV or radio to catch up on the day's news. Instead, use this quiet morning time to think.

Now it's most likely that when you do sit still and quiet and try to concentrate on life's important questions, you will run into another distraction — internal noise. This is the noise within your own head, nagging thoughts about paying the bills, getting the groceries, the day ahead at work. When you fill your mind with the relatively mundane thoughts and actions of everyday living, you become your own worst interruption. Trivial thoughts and concerns become a constant distraction from self-examination, creating an internal cacophony that drowns out serious contemplation.

"The horse which is my mind flies like the wind," wrote Tibetan poet Jetsun Milarepa. When you think of how quickly your mind can race from one thought to another, you realize how true this comparison is. Yet, like a horse, the mind can be tamed and taught. When you can do that, you can create your own retreat wherever you are.

So how do you train your stubborn, undisciplined mind? There are many techniques. One I recommend, especially for beginners, is visualization. Sit in a comfortable position and close your eyes. Then see yourself going through your day, as slowly as possible. See yourself getting out of bed, getting dressed, eating breakfast, brushing your teeth, walking to the bus stop, and so on. Take the time to notice things you usually don't. Think about why you do the things you do. Think about what makes you who you are. Or you can just concentrate on your breathing, hearing and feeling the air come into your nostrils and go back out—in and out, in a steady rhythm.

What usually happens the first time someone tries these techniques is that they fall asleep—and that's OK. It is relaxing to be seated comfortably and to experience quiet with no distractions. It's only natural that you would feel sleepy. But regardless of whether you fall asleep or get distracted or just can't concentrate, it's not a failure. Don't punish yourself and don't give up. Just try again another time or use another technique.

"The mind is like a lake, and every stone that drops into it raises waves," observed Swami Vivekananda, the meditation master who lived in the late nineteenth century century, in his *Meditation According to Yoga*. "These waves do not let us see what we are. The full moon is reflected in the water of the lake, but the surface is so disturbed that we do not see the reflection clearly. Let it be calm. Do not let nature raise the wave. Keep quiet and then after a little while she will give you up. Then we know what we are."

However, we cannot calm the waters of the mind by trying not to think of something very specific. If you've ever tried not to think of something—like the last piece of cake when you are trying to lose weight—you know that is often the worst choice you can make. The more you try to block a certain thought, the more stubbornly it forces its way in. Pretty soon all you can think about is how good that last piece of cake would taste and how you really deserve a treat for being good about your diet most of the time and how you could work off the extra calories on the treadmill later on.

Why is that? You can't get the thought of the cake out of your mind because you have become caught up in it emotionally. The cake has become more than just a piece of food. In your mind, it has become something you deserve but are being denied. You have wrapped up part of your identity with the piece of cake.

That's the way it is with most distracting thoughts. So if you can't block or ignore such thoughts, how do you keep them from distracting you? There is a story told about Buddha and one of his students that explains the attitude you should take.

One day Buddha and his student were taking a long, hot walk in the countryside. They walked through a small stream and met an oxcart about to cross the stream in the opposite direction. Soon Buddha and his student reached a tree and stopped to rest in its shade. Buddha asked his student to go back down to the little stream to get some water to drink. The student went back to the stream, but saw that it was clouded with mud and returned quickly to Buddha to tell him the water was too muddy to drink. But Buddha told him to go back to the stream and wait, giving him instructions not to poke or stir the water. The student did as he was asked, simply sitting by the stream and watching its cloudy swirls. Soon he noticed that the mud began to settle back to the bottom, leaving the water clear and pure again. He realized that the oxcart they passed must have churned up the bottom of the stream and made the water muddy. He then scooped up a cup of the now clear water and returned joyfully to his teacher.

Taking the water gratefully, Buddha explained to his student that distracting thoughts in our mind cloud our consciousness the same way the oxcart muddied the stream. But if we just acknowledge these thoughts and feelings silently, without dwelling on them, then they will go away on their own, just as the student sat quietly and watched as the disturbed stream settled back to its clear state.

This practice of sitting still and quietly is meditation. How you meditate, as I said, will be up to you, although most people find it helpful to choose a quiet spot and a quiet time of day for their practice. The important thing is to begin to meditate regularly, every day, even if it's just for a few minutes at first. If you wait until your life slows down a little or you have more time, you will never begin. As the Tibetan yogi Milarepa said, "The affairs of the world will go on forever. Do not delay the practice of meditation." By practicing daily, meditation becomes a habit.

The aim of meditation is to achieve tranquility of mind, so silence is very important. "Learn silence," as Greek mathematician and philosopher Pythagoras said. "With the quiet serenity of a meditative mind, listen, absorb, transcribe, and transform."

When is your life the quietest? I'm not talkative in the morning anyway, so I use that time for my meditation. My phone, my computer, and my TV are all turned off. But if you have young children you need to get to school each morning, you may need to get up earlier or wait until the children go to sleep to enjoy your quiet time. Or you may be able to slip away for a meditative lunch break.

I enjoy silence, and that makes it easier for me to meditate. If you don't like silence or feel uneasy when your surroundings are too quiet, then meditation will be uncomfortable for you at first. But just keep practicing, a little more each day, and gradually you will learn to appreciate the joy of silence. "Your thoughts are nothing but words. Words are noisy. Can your being be wordless?" asks Swami Sukhobodhananda. "Then see the magic of silence happening in you. This is meditation."

With regular practice you will grow more comfortable with your particular meditation style and it will become a natural part of you. An accomplished actor or dancer makes each performance look effortless, yet hours and hours of training and practice went into that "effortless" performance. The same is true of meditation. Those who have practiced for many years make it look easy, but that ease did not come overnight.

Here's another truth about meditation: Unless you integrate the insight you gain in your daily meditation into the rest of your life, it is a waste of time. There is a story of a man who approached a famous yogi with a complaint. "Master, I have been meditating for fifteen years now, and it has brought no change in my life."

"Oh, really?" the yogi asked. "How much time do you spend meditating, my son?"

"Thirty minutes," he said rather proudly. "And I do it every day, without fail."

"That is really remarkable," the yogi congratulated him. "But what do you do in the remaining twenty-three and a half hours?"

You see, meditation is not the answer in and of itself. Meditation is just the process you use to bring peace, serenity, and happiness into all aspects of your life—not just for thirty minutes or an hour at a time. People often complain of a shortage of time and money, but if they slowed down a bit and paid attention to the small but important aspects of life that don't revolve around money, they would be happier. Meditation helps you make that realization.

In one story a student asked a Zen master how he used his meditation in his life.

"In my sleeping and my eating," the master replied.

The student was puzzled. "Everyone sleeps and eats," he said.

The master nodded and said, "But when it is time to sleep, I sleep. When it is time to eat, I eat."

What the Zen master was saying was that, because of his meditation, he was so in touch with the rhythms of his life that he knew exactly what he should be doing and when he should be doing it. He was fully conscious, self-aware, and living in the moment each second of his life. His mind and his body were relaxed and calm, totally connected and in harmony. This should also be our goal.

Some people find it easier to calm their mind if their bodies are in gentle motion. I practice yoga myself every day. Yoga is a time-honored meditative practice in which breathing techniques and physical poses combine to relax the body and calm the mind. Depending on the technique, you may be asked to focus your thoughts on a particular subject or to chant a mantra or to concentrate on your breathing. There are many different techniques and schools of thought for both meditation and yoga, too many to mention here.

Whether you find your inner peace through meditation, yoga, or something else, remember to practice it daily and to integrate it fully into your life. As the Chinese proverb says, "The man who removes a mountain begins by carrying away small stones." You won't move the mountain of mental distractions in your life in one day, but you can decrease its size a little at a time.

And when you do unplug from life's distractions and turn your vision inward, the rewards are great. "In the attitude of silence the soul finds the path in a clearer light, and what is elusive and deceptive resolves itself into crystal clearness," Gandhi said.

Most importantly, when you develop the habit of silence, you will find your mind is open to experience the deep joy of true happiness. By remaining still and silent, you will achieve what you can never reach by endless searching. "Happiness is a butterfly, which when pursued, is always just beyond your grasp," wrote American author Nathaniel Hawthorne, "but which, if you will sit down quietly, may alight upon you."

Checklist:

Take a few minutes to determine where you are on the happiness scale right now, on a scale of one to ten.

Now meditate for a while on these questions:

- What are t he distractions in my life?

- How can I enjoy *this* moment in life and stop thinking of the next?

- How can I turn down the volume in my life?

- How can I make every day a "retreat" while staying in place?

Reminder for today:

Today I will meditate and attain a tranquil mind.

4

The Magic and Mystery of Simplicity

All wonders you seek are within yourself.

— SIR THOMAS BROWNE

learned a great deal about simplicity during the summers of my twelfth and thirteenth years. When I was growing up in India, each summer we got two months holiday from school. For two summers in a row, my father let me accompany a monk, or saint, as we called him, and his followers as they went from village to village. These happy men carried all their worldly possessions in one tiny bag. Each day, they chanted and prayed and meditated upon the higher issues of self-discovery. When they came to a village, the head monk gave one or two discourses daily.

The talks were heavily attended by the villagers, who lived in simple mud huts and had not much more than the monks, but always brought offerings to the monks.

The way the monks lived their lives made a big impression on me. The whole time I was with them, I never felt like I was missing out on anything at all. We never worried that we would go hungry or not have a place to sleep. Our needs were always met.

I still lived a fairly simple life when I first came to the United States. I arrived with all my belongings in one suitcase. But I found to fit in the business world here, I needed to buy a suit. And so it began. First I bought a suit, then more clothes, then a car and a house and possessions to fill it. I told myself my desires were actually needs and began to accumulate more and more. By the time I returned to India for a visit, I had saved ten thousand dollars—the amount I told my father I would need to return to India permanently. But now that I had been infected by the virus of desire, that didn't seem like enough money anymore. The young boy with no possessions who could tag along with holy men and happily beg for his meals had become a young man ruled by desires. In a sense my possessions owned me instead of the other way around. My new possessions enveloped me and made it hard for me to see what was really important, the divinity inside me.

One way the ancient Greeks visualized a person's true nature was as a golden figurine covered by layers of cheap pottery. That is, what people can see of us—our bodies, our possessions, our jobs—aren't really us. The figurative chipping away of this base exterior to reveal your true nature is called "eudemonia" —from the Greek *eu* ("good") and *daimon* ("spirit" or "deity")—and was considered by the Greek philosopher Aristotle to be the noblest goal in life.

In his Yoga Sutras, the ancient sage Patanjali says that ignorance of one's true nature is the root cause of unhappiness. This ignorance leads to egoism, when a person seeks personal gratification at all costs. Interestingly, Patanjali says this can take the form of either attachment to the things of the world or aversion to the things of the world. Neither extreme leads to happiness. Instead, egoism leads to an unhealthy fear of death.

The way to break down egoism and ignorance is by experiencing "the light of understanding that come from regular and persistent practice of yoga," according to the introduction to Swami Satyananda Saraswati's commentary on the Yoga Sutras.

In the previous chapter, we discussed how you can begin this process by turning down the volume in your life and focusing your thoughts through meditative practices. In these times of contemplation, you become more self-aware and begin to glimpse that golden figure within you. But to experience happiness, you must be in touch with its source, your true nature, and so must chip away at all those impediments wrapped around it. Like the monks, you must simplify your life by curbing your desires. You don't need to rid yourself of all your possessions, but you need to become emotionally detached from them. Remember that you own your material goods and not the other way around.

In the movie *Wall Street*, actor Michael Douglas delivers this line: "Greed is good." Well, greed is *not* good. In fact, it is one of the enemies of happiness. Like the other happiness enemies mentioned before—anger, pride, jealousy, and pleasure-seeking—greed is the result of inappropriate desires in our life. A hedonistic, pleasure-seeking lifestyle is like throwing gasoline on the unquenchable fires of desire. Desire is a good thing when it is directed at a worthy goal: truth, justice, equality. But focused on unworthy goals, desire leads to frustration, disappointment, bitterness. If you don't believe me, look at what happened to those people on Wall Street who let their greed run rampant and nearly brought this country to its knees economically. Look at the heartbreak and suffering that led to, not just for them, but also for the rest of the country, and then tell me what's good about greed.

In America, for the most part, we are free to pursue whichever career path we wish. The promise of America is that, with hard work, you can achieve as much as you want. And while that attitude has led to innovative inventions, creative entrepreneurial ventures, and immense wealth, it has also made Americans particularly susceptible to the virus of desires. Consumer demand for the latest gadgets and the newest fashions drives the economy, so we are constantly being assaulted by temptations. TV and Internet advertising entice us to try new foods, to pamper ourselves, to buy more clothes, furniture, jewelry, appliances, and so on that we don't need and can't afford. Our neighbors get a new car or go on a fabulous vacation, and we want the same thing — or something better.

Sometimes we only desire something because other people want it too. This is how crazes start, when absolutely everyone has to have the newest toy, like the iPhone when it was first introduced. As Alexander Pope wrote, long before the advent of TV commercials and pop-up advertising, "Man never thinks himself happy, but when he enjoys those things which others want or desire."

Turning down the volume in our lives is one way to minimize the effects of these temptations. The less we see or hear of these suggestive messages, the better we are able to resist their temptation. This is a situation in which silence — turning off the television, the radio, the computer — can be an ally. "It is much easier to suppress a first desire than to satisfy those that follow" was the wise advice of Benjamin Franklin, one of America's founding fathers.

But we cannot solve the problem of desire purely externally. Remember: The problem is you. The solution is you. We need to work from the inside to curb our desires. We can do that by paying *less* attention to temptation and *more* attention to our response to it.

The next time you are tempted to buy something, pause for a moment to ask yourself, "Is this something I really need or just something I want?" Nine times out of ten, it will be the latter. Then go on to ask yourself why you want this particular item. At first you may think, "Because it makes me happy." But now you know where true happiness is, so what this object gives you is not happiness but pleasure.

So what's wrong with pleasure? Nothing, if you want to spend your life on the hedonic treadmill, continually chasing after your next desire. But if your goal is true happiness, then these pleasures are destructive to that purpose. While we think following our desires for money, success, possessions, and even love will lead to happiness, they do not. In fact, when those desires are not fulfilled, they create even more negativity: anger, jealousy, depression.

That's because the very nature of a desire is that it remains forever unfulfilled. By definition, it is a want, a longing. The difference between true happiness and desire is like the difference between water and a soft drink. One quenches thirst while the other fuels it. How else could soda manufacturers make their millions?

One of the best-known stories about this sort of unquenchable desire is "The Fisherman and His Wife," from the Brothers Grimm. In the story, a poor fisherman who lives with his wife in a wretched hovel catches a magical talking fish and lets him go. When he tells his wife, she is furious with him and demands that he return to the sea and ask the fish for a favor — to turn their hovel into a nice cottage. The fish grants the wish, and the couple is happy for a while. But then the wife grows restless and wants a castle, then a palace, then a kingdom, then an empire. The magical fish grants the wish each time, but the wife can never be content. "Her desires would not let her sleep," the Grimm Brothers write. "She kept thinking what she wanted to become next."

Finally the wife declares that she wants to be like God, to be able to tell the sun and moon when to rise and when to set. When the terrified fisherman makes this awful request of the fish, the ocean erupts in a huge storm, and the fisherman returns home to find his wife back in their original wretched hovel. Because of her insatiable desire, the wife lost everything. Not only that, but she was never happy with her life, even when she ruled an empire, because her desires kept leading her higher, making her hungry for what else she might become instead of being content with what she had.

The story of the fisherman's wife also shows us that it's not just a desire for material possessions that can come between us and true happiness. She was also hungry for power. For others, the desire that rules their lives might be for wealth, glory, fame, or luxury. We all have basic needs for shelter, food, and drink as well as for the respect and love of others. But when our desire for creature comforts far exceeds our needs, or our desire to succeed blinds us to what we already have, then those desires are harmful.

You don't have to be a monk or a hermit to live a simple life. In fact, one of the best examples of the simple life is being led by a successful, famous musician whom I met many years ago. When I first saw folksinger Pete Seeger, I had no idea how famous he was. He dressed simply, spoke kindly to strangers, and readily agreed to perform at a fund-raiser I was planning. It wasn't until I was printing up flyers for the show and people began to get excited that I realized just how well-known this composer of "Where Have All the Flowers Gone?" and "If I Had a Hammer" and many other songs was. He performed a concert to a packed house.

Later on we went to visit Peter and his wife, Toshi, in New York State. They lived in the simplest of cabins that they had built themselves. He chopped his own wood, and they didn't have electricity. Yet they were as happy as royalty, and I imagine they still are today, because they didn't let the trimmings and trappings of fame distract them from what was truly important in their lives — music and social activism.

Now, I don't expect you to beg for your bread or even chop your own wood. But you will be happier if you simplify your life as much as you can.

Sometimes we make our lives needlessly complicated just because we assume that we need to have what everyone else has, to "keep up with the Joneses." We don't take the time to consider other options. For example, do you really need two cars or could you get by with just one by taking the bus or carpooling with co-workers or neighbors? Do you really need five hundred TV channels or could you live with a basic package or even without television at all? Do you really need to buy a fancy coffee shop drink every morning or would you be better off making a pot of coffee at home?

The list goes on. I bet you'll be surprised how many things you can get rid of and yet never miss. And just as the hedonic wheel carries you on an upward spiral, a simpler lifestyle leads you back down. As you reduce your desires, your life will become calmer, more focused. You'll be spending less money, so you won't have to work longer hours to pay your bills. And you won't be spending as much time shopping because you'll be buying less.

Instead, you'll have more time to spend with your family and for other activities you were too busy to enjoy before.

Incorporating the magic and mystery of simplicity into your everyday life will improve your well-being in so many ways. You will gain so much more than you lose, and that is the proper way to approach simplifying your life. Less is more.

For example, cutting back on the number of times you eat out will lead to healthier meals that you prepare at home and time to sit around the dinner table and talk about your day. Sharing the duties of cooking and cleaning up will teach children valuable skills and make mealtime more enjoyable for the adults. When you reduce the amount of money you spend on entertainment, you open yourself up to the possibilities of inexpensive or even free ways to have fun. Perhaps you'll start a family game night or go on regular walks or bike rides. Maybe you'll even join your neighbors for a potluck meal and an evening of charades or music or outdoor games.

When you simplify your life, you will have less stress and fewer worries. Almost everyone you meet complains about how much stress they are under at work or at home. But when you think about it, most stress is self-inflicted. That is, we have expectations that are too high. When we don't perform up to our own standards, or we don't get everything accomplished that we think we should, we feel frustrated. Our reality and our ideal don't match up. We keep falling short.

But what if you lowered your expectations of yourself a bit? You are not superhuman, after all. And even superhumans couldn't do everything we expect ourselves to be able to do in a twenty-four-hour day: be the perfect employee, spouse, parent, and community member. Instead of spreading yourself so thin, concentrate on what is really important to you and what brings you the most satisfaction, and invest yourself in that.

If you still aren't convinced, think of simplifying your life as a way of paying yourself a bonus in one of the most valuable commodities of all: time. Think of all the time- and labor-saving devices that have been invented so that we could enjoy so much more leisure time than our ancestors ever had—lawnmowers, dishwashers, microwave ovens, computers, and so on. Yet what do we do with all this so-called leisure time?

When you simplify your life, you will have more time to enjoy it. The saying isn't "Run as fast as you can and smell the roses." It's "Stop and smell the roses." You will begin to appreciate what's truly important in life, like watching your children grow up, sitting quietly and holding your spouse's hand, listening to the summer rain gently hitting your roof. And whenever you look back on the way you lived before, you will wonder what it was that you were always so busy doing and why.

Even when your work is saving lives, you can overdo it and jeopardize your home life. Dr. Allan Hamilton, gifted neurosurgeon and author of *The Scalpel and the Soul*, tells a story about his son, now an adult, when he was eight years old. At the time Dr. Hamilton was such a busy surgeon that he practically lived at the hospital. One morning his young son told him, "I wish I had a tumor in my brain." When the perplexed surgeon asked him why he would say such a terrible thing, the son replied, "That way I could spend more time with you." Because of the impact of that statement from his son so long ago, the doctor to this day does a better job of balancing his work and family life.

Few things are more difficult than to lead a life of overwhelming simplicity. Words can never do justice to describe the simple lives successfully lived by Gandhi, Mother Teresa, Thoreau, and other pioneering great souls.

Most of the writers describe the iconic details of their dwelling and skeletal possessions because that is all a product of materialistic culture writers can see.

The heart and soul of simplicity is its easy and unassuming yet highly pervading presence. Anyone can wear the loincloth and imitate Gandhi, but only a lucky soul after a great deal of toil can cultivate the necessary habits for the emergence of simplicity.

No classes or coaching camps can teach you to learn simplicity. Its growth is spontaneous when we create the right conditions. Just as a farmer prepares the ground before he plants a seed, we have to create the necessary conditions and environment to spur the growth of simplicity. The cultivation of the following habits in our day-to-day life can create the necessary conditions: nonviolence, truth, fearlessness, purity of heart, humility, patience, detachment from objects, uprightness, even temper, spirit of renunciation, quietude, gentle speech, tenderness, and self-denial of physical desires.

Living simply may not be easy at first. But as with the other principles of this book, it can be done by incorporating certain habits into your life each day. And in this case, it will also be necessary to unlearn some of the habits you already have. You will need to learn to ignore or avoid temptations in the form of advertising while at the same time becoming mindful of what you are spending money on and why. Set certain rules for yourself, like sticking to a weekly budget. Reduce the number of credit cards you have or stop using them altogether. If you don't have the cash to pay for it, don't buy it. Each morning, set a goal for yourself for the day not to buy anything new (beyond the most basic groceries or supplies) or that if you do buy anything new, you have to get rid of something you already own.

The sooner we can accept that our true nature — that elusive golden image at our core — is the source of true happiness, the easier it is to remove those layers of ugly desires and impediments hiding it. You will begin to learn contentment as you free yourself from the bondage of desire. As the Greek Stoic philosopher Epictetus said, "Freedom is not procured by a full enjoyment of what is desired, but by controlling the desire." And at last you will know how those monks I traveled with in my youth could be so happy carrying all their possessions in one tiny bag.

Checklist:

Take a few minutes to determine where you are on the happiness scale right now, on a scale of one to ten.

Now meditate for a while on these questions:

- What is the biggest impediment to your happiness?

- What can you do to chip away at it?

- How can you curb your desires for more and learn to live within (or far below) your means?

Reminder for today:

Today I will conquer the enemies of happiness— desires, anger, delusion, greed, guilt, attachment, deception, jealousy, and most of all, ego.

5

Compassion Increases Happiness

Do unto others as you would have them do unto you.

— *Luke 6:31*

(The Golden Rule)

As a gift my wife surprised me with a membership to a newly built health complex. I go regularly; in fact, because I rise so early each morning, I am often the first one there. When I finish with my workout, I get a towel to pat away my perspiration. Then I take a stack of towels and go to the other patrons who have arrived by then and give a towel to each of them and say good morning.

The effect is truly amazing. The people at my gym are generally serious about their workouts, concentrating hard on bicycle riding or treadmill running. But when I offer them a towel, they immediately start to smile. They say thank you and wish me a good day. I feel better too, just knowing that I help their morning get off to a better start. The whole exchange cost me very little—a few minutes of my time, a few extra steps in the gym—yet it brings such happiness to us all. Even people I have never met before become friends in a short period.

Now I know and they know that they are all perfectly capable of getting their own towels. But they are always touched by the thought that someone else, someone they may not even know that well, has gone to the effort to do it for them, without being asked. Why do I do it? It is just one way I like to practice the Golden Rule. I have quoted the Christian version above, but the same thought is expressed in nearly every other major religion. In Islam, the saying goes, "No one of you is a believer until he desires for his brother that which he desires for himself." The Jewish Talmud expresses it this way: "What is hateful to you, do not do to your fellow man. This is the entire Law; all the rest is commentary." Those of the Hindu faith believe, "This is the sum of duty; do naught onto others what you would not have them do unto you."

So far in the book, I have focused on the personal, individual experience of happiness. I have said that happiness is you, that the problem is you, and the solution is you. But I have also talked about the importance of incorporating the habit of happiness into your daily life, and that daily life includes your interactions with other people. This is not a contradiction if you recognize that the source of happiness, that divinity within you, is the same for everyone.

To take the imagery I borrowed from the ancient Greeks in the last chapter a step further, we may all be covered in different types of pottery, but we share the same golden core. That's why the Golden Rule is such a sensible and widespread moral code. If we all share the same divinity, the same source within us, then of course we should treat each other well. Otherwise, we're mistreating ourselves.

In order to practice the Golden Rule in your daily life, you need to develop both empathy and compassion. Empathy is being able to put yourself in another person's place, to see the world through someone else's eyes. Compassion is responding to that experience, treating another the way you would want to be treated if you were in the same situation. In my simple example, because I have been working out, I empathize with the other patrons of the gym who are also sweaty. I show my compassion by offering them a towel because that is what I would want in their situation.

Very closely related to the Golden Rule is Mahatma Gandhi's wise message, "You must be the change you want to see in the world." Now this doesn't mean that overnight one person can right all the wrongs of this world. What it means is that the change begins with you. You don't have to wait until you are famous or you have traveled the world or you have written a book. The change begins wherever you are, whenever you start. If you want to be respected, then respect others. If you want to be loved, then love others. If you want to be happy, then bring happiness to others. Have you ever noticed how contagious a smile is? Try it sometime. Just smile pleasantly at the next person you pass in the hallway or on the street and watch the reaction. His face will soften for a second and he may even return your smile. He might even say hello.

Let me make an important point here about your happiness and others. The goal of this book is to help you see that you possess *within yourself* all that you need to be happy, that your happiness does not depend upon anyone or anything else in your life. I repeat this because I have seen so many people who chase unsuccessfully after happiness because they believe if they only had the love of a certain person or a prestigious job or a million dollars, then they would be happy. None of these brings you happiness because they are all external to you.

But notice the difference between making your happiness dependent upon someone else and inviting that person to share in your happiness journey. In the first you place impossible demands on the other person. In the second you are asking nothing of them, only offering of yourself.

In my talks, I often say, "Happiness is not a team sport." That's because I want to emphasize that happiness is you and not to be found in something or someone external to you. Instead, if you think of happiness as a sport, it is more like golf — an individual pursuit that can be more enjoyable in the company of others. You can use your solo game to work on the problems you know you have, but when you play with others, they may be able to spot something you're not aware of — a problem in your stance, for example — and may be able to offer you tips to improve. And you can do the same for them. It's only practical that if we involve those closest to us in our happiness journey, their support will lift us up and increase their own happiness as well.

One of my friends suggested the idea of having a "happiness buddy," and I think that's a wonderful idea. After all, there is a support group out there for all the negatives in this world — addiction, illness, abuse — why not a support group for something positive? You and your "happiness buddy" could read the book together, compare notes, share what works for you. You may want to share activities suggested in the book, like meditation or yoga, or you may just want to set aside a time each day to talk. Ask each other for observations because others are sometimes better at seeing changes in us than we see in ourselves. Share any difficulties you have been having in case she has some insight or a different perspective. You may want to get the whole family or your office or your civic club involved, to make it sort of a "happiness project."

You must be careful, however, in inviting others to join you on your happiness journey. It must be an open invitation with no pressure to accept, no punishment if declined. Just as no one else can make you happy, you can't force happiness on anyone else, no matter how good your intentions are. In fact, you probably will get just the opposite effect from the one you want. To successfully recruit others to join your journey, you may need to be a little sneaky.

Here's what I mean: Imagine if the cook in your family one day announced, "The doctor says I need to go on a low-sodium diet, so no more salt in any of our food." Immediately the complaints would begin about the bland, boring diet being forced on the family, and mealtimes would become dreary and disappointing. But what if the cook is a bit slyer and doesn't mention the new diet to anyone? What if he or she begins preparing a separate, tasty, low-sodium dish for one and serves the regular fare to everyone else? When the others notice the difference, the cook admits it is low-sodium, but doesn't want to make them eat it. They can have a taste, though, if they want. As the low-sodium dishes begin to look more and more delicious, the family wants to try them too. After a while, they insist to the cook that there's no need to fix two separate meals, that they'll go on the low-sodium diet too.

The wise cook has led by example, not by force. This brings us back to Gandhi's message to "be the change" and to the Golden Rule. Once others see the happiness within you in action, they will want to be part of it. When they see a difference in you, they will be eager to find out how their lives can be different too.

The best place to start practicing the Golden Rule is at home, with the ones you love. If you like being listened to, then take the time to really listen to your spouse when he or she tells you about the day. Resist the temptation to share your own stories or to give advice until your spouse has finished speaking. Just listen. The same goes for your children.

It's important to make this extra effort to communicate, face to face. Ironically, as the world gets more and more connected by technology, we have a harder and harder time communicating with each other. In her book, *Alone Together*, Sherry Turkle of MIT writes, "We expect more from technology and less from each other." We don't express our true emotions to each other. "We aren't 'happy' anymore: we're simply a semicolon followed by a parenthesis. Instead of talking on the phone, we send a text; instead of writing wistful letters, we edit our Tumblr blog."

Even worse, technology can distract us from the people who are right next to us. Don't keep checking your phone or your computer for messages when the person you are with is talking. Put other activities aside for at least a few minutes and listen to what they are saying. You might be surprised.

Don't use the Golden Rule as an excuse to criticize or to control others. This is particularly tempting within your own home, where "father knows best." Because you know them so well, you may think you already know what your spouse or child or sibling or parent needs — and you're not afraid to tell them so. But with those closest to you, it is especially important that you take the time to put yourself in their place, not yours, and see the world through their eyes. Remember what it felt like when you were a teenager and how deeply it hurt when your best friend snubbed you. Imagine what it must be like to be as old as your parents and not being able to do all the things that you once took for granted, like driving. Because you love them, you want to rush in to solve their problems for them, to do what you think is best for them. But this isn't necessarily what they want or even what they need. It may be hard at first, but make yourself listen to what they say and wait for them to tell you what they want from you.

"Being the change" creates a ripple effect in your world. What starts with you and the ones closest to you spreads outward. When you've practiced the Golden Rule with your family for a while, try it with your friends, then with your work colleagues, acquaintances, neighbors, and even strangers.

Naturally, it will be easier to practice the Golden Rule with people who are already familiar to you or like you. What takes more effort is putting yourself in the place of someone different from you and responding with kindness. Let's say you go to a diner for breakfast and the service is incredibly slow. Your waitress is nice enough, but seems distracted and confused. After thirty minutes with only one cold cup of coffee to show for it, you are ready to walk out. You keep looking at your watch, calculating whether you will be late for your next appointment if you keep waiting. Then the waitress shows up at your table with your breakfast and yet another apology. "I don't usually work the morning shift," she says. "I worked late last night and the boss called me in because the morning waitress slipped on the ice this morning and broke her leg."

How do you respond to this information? Are you still angry because of the inconvenience the waitress's slowness has caused you? Or can you put yourself in her place for a minute—a tired server pulling a double shift because of an unfortunate accident?

Another way the Golden Rule is expressed is to "love your neighbor as yourself." In the Christian Bible, when Jesus tells this rule to his followers, one of them asks, "Who is my neighbor?" Instead of answering directly, he tells the story of the Good Samaritan, in which a man who has been beaten and left for dead by robbers is neglected and ignored by his own countrymen but cared for tenderly by one who would normally be his enemy. Substitute "Palestinian and Israeli," "Serb and Croat," "Hutu and Tutsi," and so on for the injured man and his rescuer, and you begin to realize how profoundly this story illustrates the Golden Rule.

The odds are you won't find a person beaten and bleeding on the side of the road, as the Good Samaritan did, but you might be surprised how often you encounter people who need help, if only your eyes and mind are open to recognizing them. Perhaps an elderly woman is struggling with getting her grocery bags into her car. Or maybe you are in a park and you hear a child crying and no one else is around. All too often, in our litigious, overly cautious world, we turn away from such sights, afraid that we will offend the elderly lady if we offer to help or be accused of hurting the child ourselves if we approach. But look into your heart and you will know the right thing to do.

One important distinction to make, though, is that what you offer someone in need isn't *your* idea of help, but *theirs*. When your daughter is in tears because her first boyfriend broke her heart, that is not the time to lecture her about how she is too young to have a serious boyfriend anyway.

She doesn't need to hear that. Instead, she just wants you to hold her and let her cry. Similarly, when your best friend does nothing but complain about her husband to you, she isn't actually expecting you to give her the name of a good therapist or a good lawyer, even though that may be what she needs. She may just be looking for your reassurance that she deserves better treatment. Sometimes what a person needs is obvious and sometimes your instincts will lead you to the right answer. But if you still don't know exactly what someone needs, rather than turning away and offering nothing, at least take the time to say, "You seem to be in trouble. How can I help?"

This process will come more naturally to you as you become comfortable with the concept of the divinity within us all. Then when you see the fear in someone else's eyes or hear the frustration in his voice, you will recognize it as your own fear, your own frustration.

Think of the Golden Rule as your 24/7 responsibility. You are never off-duty where courtesy and kindness are concerned. Keep your eyes and ears open for opportunities to put the rule in practice. When you are driving, for example, don't be so intent on getting where you're going that you forget that others have the same concerns. Be courteous and when safety allows, allow others to merge in the flow of traffic rather than cutting them off. On the bus don't bury your head in a book and ignore the people who are standing. Instead, offer your seat to a child or a senior or anyone with heavy bags. When walking, instead of charging through doorways first or letting a door slam shut on the person behind you, hold doors open for others.

Let empathy and compassion guide your interactions with others all day, all the time. A movement started a few years back called "Random Acts of Kindness" encouraged people to do good deeds anonymously for strangers—like putting extra quarters in parking meters—or to write a note of appreciation for someone who helped them in life.

There's no doubt that if you practice the Golden Rule each day, you will bring moments of happiness into the lives of others. But just as important, these simple acts will also reveal to you the happiness within yourself. The intent of the Golden Rule is not to sacrifice yourself for the sake of others. It is to increase the happiness of all, including yourself. Remember the assumption behind "love your neighbor as you love yourself" is that you first love yourself! For, if you don't love yourself, how can you love others? When you love your neighbor and make the Golden Rule a daily habit, you will feel more confident, more assured that you are a good person who does good things, a person who deserves to be happy, a person who is content. And you will know more than ever that happiness is you.

Checklist:

Take a few minutes to determine where you are on the happiness scale right now, on a scale of one to ten.

Now meditate for a while on these questions:

- What does the Golden Rule mean to you?

- How can you develop greater empathy and compassion for others?

- Do you want to invite someone to accompany you on your happiness journey? If so, who would it be and how would you invite them?

Reminder for today:

Today I will not judge anyone by his appearance, and I will treat everyone as I want to be treated.

6

Work Is Worship

The American Dream is that dream of a land in which life should be better and richer and fuller for everyone, with opportunity for each according to ability or achievement.... It is not a dream of motor cars and high wages merely, but a dream of social order in which each man and each woman shall be able to attain to the fullest stature of which they are innately capable, and be recognized by others for what they are, regardless of the fortuitous circumstances of birth or position.

— JAMES TRUSLOW ADAMS, THE EPIC OF AMERICA

T he reason that so many other immigrants, including me, have come to America over the years is the promise that if you work hard enough, you can be a success. In this country you are not born into a caste system that restricts your upward mobility. Here you are not judged by the color of your skin, your religious background, your national origin, your gender, or any other factor except whether you can get the job done.

At least that is the ideal that we strive for. From the beginning, settlers have come to these shores seeking a better life. The founders of Jamestown were looking for gold and found a golden leaf instead to make their fortunes. The Pilgrims sought the freedom to practice a religion outside the one sanctioned by the government. Both groups brought with them a strong work ethic. In Virginia the work was entrepreneurial—clearing land, growing crops, establishing trade relationships—while in New England, work was a Puritan virtue that was good for the soul. Even the French writer Voltaire, certainly no Puritan, recognized the virtue of work: "Work spares us from three evils: boredom, vice and need."

These positive attitudes that the founders of this country had toward work combined over the years to create an American society that makes employment a top priority. We praise those who put in extra hours and look with suspicion on those who don't have jobs. We are even wary of vacation time, taking far less time off from our jobs than in most other developed nations. It is said that while Europeans, for example, work to live, Americans live to work. When we meet someone new, right away we ask, "What do you do?" and we introduce ourselves to others in terms of our jobs: "I am a doctor." "I am an engineer." "I build websites."

At times of economic growth and vitality, this emphasis on hard work seems to be the key to happiness. Work hard enough and you can achieve the American dream, the same promise that attracted me in my youth.

In times of economic hardship, the opposite may be true — that is, the happiness of workers may be what determines how hard they work. In a recent opinion piece in the *New York Times*, a Harvard professor and an independent researcher concluded that happier people did work harder than others at their jobs. But what seems to be surprising to 95 percent of managers is that traditional motivational tools such as raises and promotions aren't what make workers the happiest. Instead, it's progress in meaningful work. "Working adults spend more of their waking hours at work than anywhere else. Work should ennoble, not kill, the human spirit," they write. When managers fail to provide or articulate the meaning and importance of the work, their employees check out mentally, what the researchers called the "disengagement crisis."

But when an employee is fully engaged in work, the company benefits and so does the worker. The happiest employees are those who feel inspired by what they do, who are passionate about their work, and who feel empowered to take on more responsibility for getting the job done.

I have done well for myself financially, but the true reward of my job teaching at a university has been the joy I received from my students. That's because work for me is not just a paycheck, but also a form of worship. By sharing my knowledge with others, I feel I am doing something that's beneficial to mankind. I haven't taught for the last five years, yet when I was in the hospital with double pneumonia, the most calls and flowers I received were from my students, some from as far back as thirty-five or forty years ago. The highest compliment I could receive were those voices telling me, "I still remember what you taught me."

Any good career counselor will tell you that the secret of success is to find something that you love to do so much that you would do it for free—then figure out a way to get paid for it. "Do not hire a man who does your work for money," advised Henry David Thoreau, "but him who does it for love of it." I didn't know I was going to be a motivational speaker, but after I realized the impact I had made on the lives of my students, I wanted to explore the potential within me to reach out to a broader audience.

Entrepreneurs have a similar attitude. While I sometimes joke that an entrepreneur is someone who will do anything rather than work a nine to five job, entrepreneurs are really those people who have figured out the unique knowledge or gift that they can bring to the world—and a way to make it pay.

Many Americans were forced to explore their entrepreneurial potential during the recent economic recession when thousands lost their jobs. Some of these unemployed workers were able to look at the loss as an opportunity to try something new, something risky. A year into the recession, the number of people who called themselves "self-employed" went up about 2.5 percent, according to the Bureau of Labor Statistics. Some invested in franchises or became direct salespeople, while others pursued their dreams by opening a business of their own. They turned their hobbies, like cooking or shooting videos, into businesses.

Vimala Rajendran was a single mother of three who was struggling to get by financially. Her friends and neighbors, who knew what a good cook she was, urged her to cater meals as a way to earn money. She built up such a following that a year ago she opened a restaurant, buoyed by $80,000 pledged by friends and neighbors, serving Indian and Southern food made from fresh, local ingredients. "When Vimala cooks, everybody eats" is her slogan. And she is serious about that. A sign posted by the door of her shop says that even those who can't pay are welcome to come inside to eat. This entrepreneur is paying forward the support she received to get her start.

People like Vimala who conquer adversity through their positive attitude illustrate the main idea of this book: Happiness is you. While you may think something as terrible as losing your job would make it impossible for you to be happy, it doesn't. That's because your job—no matter how much you identify with it—is not you. It is external to you. You are the problem and you are the solution.

There is a story told by Father Anthony de Mello, a Jesuit priest in India, called "The Way the World Is." In it, a crocodile is trapped in a net and appeals to a boy passing by to help free her. But when the boy approaches, the crocodile tries to gobble him up. The boy manages to keep the powerful jaws from closing on him and berates the crocodile, "This is how you repay my kindness?"

But the crocodile says, "Don't take it personally. This is the law of life. This is the way the world is."

The boy says he doesn't believe that, so the crocodile says he can ask any passersby what they think. A mother bird tells him how she watched a snake devour her nestlings and a donkey complains of being abandoned by his master in his old age. "This is the law of life," they agree. "This is the way the world is."

Then the boy asks a rabbit, but the rabbit says they can't discuss such an important question with the boy stuck in the crocodile's mouth like that. "But he'll run away if I let him go," the crocodile says.

"Nonsense," the rabbit says. "Why, you could kill him with one blow from your tail."

So the crocodile, not remembering that most of her body, including her tail, is still trapped in the net, lets the boy go, and the rabbit tells him to run. He also advises the boy to bring back some villagers to kill the crocodile and have a feast. The boy does just that, but his dog also comes with him, and when the dog sees the rabbit, he attacks and kills him. And the boy then realizes this *is* the way the world is.

The recession was like that too. Through no fault of their own, thousands suddenly found themselves unemployed, just as the helpful rabbit and the treacherous crocodile met the same fate in the story. Suddenly they were not only out of work, but they had also lost their very identities. Even the people who were still employed suffered from the stress of uncertainty and because they had to work even longer hours for the same pay (or less) to take the place of those who had been let go.

Yet some have been able to rise above circumstances and reshape their own destiny. What is it that makes them different? I would say it is their realization that happiness is you.

Let's look at the two major frustrations related to work: you don't have a job or you are unhappy with the job you have. The problem isn't your work or your lack of work. It's your attitude. The problem is you; the solution is you.

First, if you are unemployed, I am not trying to belittle your situation. I realize that suddenly losing your income is a serious issue. But what I want you to know is that it doesn't have to cripple you psychologically. You should take some time to grieve for your job, just as you would any important loss in your life, but you also need to move on from that grief. Recognize that you are more than your job. Take this time to explore what brings you the most joy and figure out how to do that, even if it doesn't produce an income. Studies show that those who do something, even volunteer work, while they are unemployed get hired more quickly than those who don't.

Second, if you are unhappy with your job, that doesn't mean you have to be an unhappy person. Many people have problems at work. In fact, Malcolm Forbes once said,

"If you have a job without any aggravations, you don't have a job." Depending on what bothers you most about your job, you can develop different strategies to keep it from affecting your inner happiness. And since we spend roughly one-third of our adult lives on the job, it's worth the investment.

Let's say you feel you are stuck in a job that is beneath you. At the height of the civil rights movement in the 1960s, the Rev. Martin Luther King Jr. was addressing an audience of mostly black citizens who had been forced to take menial positions even when they were qualified for better jobs. And while he helped to lead the struggle for better jobs and better pay for black workers, he also encouraged his followers to take pride in their jobs, whatever they might be. "All labor that uplifts humanity has dignity and importance and should be undertaken with painstaking excellence," King told them.

In a sense he was echoing one of his key influences in nonviolent protest, Gandhi, who decades earlier had told his followers in India, "Satisfaction lies in the effort, not in the attainment, full effort is full victory." Gandhi also believed in making physical labor an integral part of life at his ashram. Every resident had jobs to do that required manual labor, including the Mahatma himself.

Doing a good job is its own reward. Maybe it would also help you to remember that many success stories had humble beginnings. Michael Dell, the founder of Dell Computers, washed dishes in a Chinese restaurant as his first job. Author Stephen King was once a janitor. Pop star Madonna worked at a Dunkin' Donuts shop.

You will also feel happier if you work to meet your own high standards and not those of other people. I take all of my motivational talks equally seriously—whether it's a weeklong corporate seminar in California or a fifteen-minute talk at the local Kiwanis Club. That's because

I take pride in my reputation, and I want to make sure that I am offering my best to whatever audience I happen to be addressing. In the same way, you should approach whatever you are doing with a goal of doing your very best. Do your work with the utmost efficiency. Work done with this attitude is a form of worship as well as its own reward. "Far and away the best prize that life has to offer is the chance to work hard at work worth doing," President Theodore Roosevelt said.

Another way to look at a low-level position is that it is a foot in the door to a better job. The story of the executive who worked his way up through the company has become a cliché, but like most clichés, it is based in truth. Bob Ulrich, former CEO of Target, worked his way up the corporate ladder starting in 1967. Brad Anderson, CEO of Best Buy, started out as a stereo salesman. And the first job Jeffrey Rein had at Walgreen's was assistant store manager. Now he's the CEO.

For some, it's not the job but the boss that they can't stand. If that's your case, turn your focus away from your supervisor and onto yourself. Do whatever you can to improve yourself and your performance. Take classes. Learn new skills. Cultivate other work relationships inside and outside your job. Perhaps you will find someone as unhappy as you are, and you can support one another by becoming "happiness buddies," as discussed in the previous chapter. With those co-workers you don't get along with or don't understand, focus on developing empathy and compassion. Once you can see your workplace through their eyes, you will better understand not only how to get along with them better, but you'll also learn to work with them to get the results you want.

If these strategies don't work for you, try taking a step back and looking at your job from a different perspective. Instead of just thinking, "What's in it for me?"

ask yourself how your work is contributing to the community at large. Develop a "How can I help you?" attitude. In the Vedic tradition, work is inherently an action, and action is an important part of the concept of karma because your actions not only have impact on this life but also in other lives to come. Consider how many lives you may touch in a single day on the job. Work is not just a way to earn money; it is a means of reaching the Almighty. Remember that your values and ethics are just as important on the job as they are at church or temple, maybe even more so.

Poet and philosopher Khalil Gibran took that notion one step further. "Work is love made visible," he wrote. "And if you cannot work with love but only with distaste, it is better that you should leave your work and sit at the gate of the temple and take alms of those who work with joy."

Approach your work with a deep, abiding faith, ever aware of the impact of your actions on others. One of my former students recently told me that he remembered something I said in 1985. That was an exhilarating yet humbling moment for me, exhilarating because I was so pleased that something I said stuck with him for so long, and humbling because it made me realize I need to make sure what I say to others is worth remembering.

In an often-quoted verse in the Bhagawad-Geeta, Lord Krishna says, "Let not the fruit of action be thy motive, nor let thy attachment be to inaction." What this means is that the real joy of any action (work) lies in doing your best — because if you truly do your best without thinking about the fruits (rewards), your actions will bring about inner purification and spiritual awakening.

What if you have already been blessed enough to retire from your job? Retirement doesn't mean your life's work is over. In many ways it has just begun. These golden years are the perfect time to increase and expand your volunteer work, or to start volunteering if you haven't before.

The key to successful volunteering is to treat it just as you would a paying job. Show up on time; do what you're asked without complaining; be pleasant and kind. Don't volunteer as if you are doing an organization a favor by just showing up. Don't come just to socialize or be seen doing good works. Don't expect to come in as the head of the board or the president of the organization just because you were a supervisor or executive in your career. Be prepared to work your way up doing menial tasks, just as you do in the business world.

Good volunteers bring the same passion and the same intensity they had for their work to their altruistic efforts. As in the business world, they are problem solvers. Some approach volunteering as social entrepreneurship. That is, they see a problem that no one else is addressing successfully and they find a solution that works. Microlending pioneer Grameen Bank in Bangladesh, for example, began as a social entrepreneurship experiment by economics professor Mohammad Yusuf, who wanted to help poor workers break the cycle of poverty and debt. He did this by making loans for amounts too small to be worthwhile for large banks, but at a small fraction of the interest charged by unscrupulous moneylenders. Yusuf was later awarded the Nobel Peace Prize for starting what became known as the microloan revolution.

Other volunteers work within an established organization to make it run more efficiently. They follow the example of Bonnie McElveen Hunter of the American Red Cross, who was so determined to trim her bloated board of directors (fifty) and simplify the board's structure that she went to Congress in 2007 to change the requirements. Charities benefit from their volunteers' experience in the business world because a charity that is run like a charity will not survive. A charity needs to run like a business, with the utmost efficiency, so that the largest percentage of money raised goes to persons in need, not to administrative costs or fund-raising. If you have a head for business and the skills to make an organization run efficiently, those are tremendous gifts to offer to any charitable group.

You might be surprised to find that Henry Ford — the great American car manufacturer, creator of the assembly line process to get work done more efficiently — had this to say about work. "There is joy in work. There is no happiness except in the realization that we have accomplished something." He obviously grasped the concept that work is integral to happiness.

Too often I hear people talk about work and spirituality as if they were two separate, even opposing, ideas. But what I've been sharing in this chapter is my belief that the two are inextricably linked, that they are one and the same. The divinity within you accompanies you to your work each day; you cannot put it in a drawer during the week and only take it out for worship services. While prayer and meditation play vital roles in our spirituality, they are not the only forms of worship. Faith requires action to thrive. St. Augustine, the early Christian philosopher, said you should "pray as though everything depended on God and work as though everything depended on you." In other words, don't just sit around expecting divine intervention to solve your problems or the world's. Take action and be the change that you seek. There is no better way to reveal the divinity within you than to display it in your actions, in your job, and in your volunteer work. Work is worship.

Checklist:

Take a few minutes to determine where you are on the happiness scale right now, on a scale of one to ten.

Now meditate for a while on these questions:

- What can you do to improve your attitude about work?

- How can you make your work better?

- How can you make your work relationships better?

Reminder for today:

Today I will have a positive attitude toward work and in all my dealings with other people.

7

Giving Is Getting

They who give have all things; they who withhold have nothing.

— *HINDU PROVERB*

I knew something was different about Sir John Templeton the very moment I met him at the local airport. In 1997 I invited him to deliver the lecture to our twenty-fifth annual stock market symposium. The founder of Templeton Mutual Funds and the Templeton Foundation gladly accepted our invitation, and when the president of my school and I went to receive Sir John, I was shocked to see an eighty-five-year-old man walking straight and carrying his own luggage. When I approached him to take his bag, he put a hand confidently on my shoulder and said, "Young man, do you really think that I am that old that I cannot carry even one piece of luggage?"

Over the next two days, I got to know Sir John better and what he told me has changed my life and outlook enormously. His life story is amazing. Sir John started his life in Tennessee, graduating from Yale and winning a Rhodes Scholarship. He went on to buy low and sell high with such success that in January 1999 *Money* magazine called him "arguably the greatest global stock picker of the century." But Sir John was also interested in spiritual and humanitarian efforts, so he established the Templeton Prize, an award of one million pounds to recognize outstanding work in the spiritual realm. Recipients have included Mother Teresa of Calcutta and evangelist Billy Graham.

What most impressed me about Sir John was that he applied the same investment strategy in every aspect of his life. His great insight and wisdom led me to call him "the swami in the three-piece suit." Investors put money into ventures that they believe will give them returns, and Sir John believed that principle held true outside of the business world as well. "Whatever it is you want, give it away," Sir John told me. "It will come back to you."

Think about that for a moment. If you want to be friends with someone, you have to approach them with friendship first. If you want someone to love you, you have to show them that you love them. If you want a person's respect, you have to treat them with respect, and so on. Peyton Conway March, the American general and army chief of staff under President Woodrow Wilson, described the situation this way: "There is a wonderful mythical law of nature that the three things we crave most in life—happiness, freedom, and peace of mind—are always attained by giving them to someone else." This is what I mean by "giving is getting," or, as St. Francis of Assisi said, "For it is in giving that we receive." The whole concept of karma is based on the notion that what you send out into the world will come back to you.

Most of what we have to give falls into one of three categories, called "the three Ts" — time, talent, and treasure. Usually it is the last *T* that we think of when we think of giving, "treasure" — monetary and material gifts. From worldwide, multimillion-dollar fund-raisers for diseases and disasters to a bag of used clothing donated to the local thrift shop, "treasure" is what we call the material things we give to others.

In America we have come to expect those who have been the most successful financially to share their treasure through charitable ventures. The government encourages philanthropy by giving generous tax breaks for charitable donations. Wealthy families such as the Kennedys, Fords, Rockefellers, and Carnegies have become nearly as famous for their philanthropy as for their riches, and today's entrepreneurs are following their example. In 1997 broadcast executive Ted Turner famously pledged one billion dollars to the United Nations, joking that "a billion's a good round number." Microsoft founder Bill Gates and his wife, Melinda, have established a foundation that seeks to encourage entrepreneurship in the fields of health and education. The software giant once observed, "I actually thought that it would be a little confusing during the same period of your life to be in one meeting when you're trying to make money, and then go to another meeting where you're giving it away." Yet that's what he's doing, to 'the tune of nearly twenty-five billion dollars in grants so far.

The Gates Foundation has specific rules for its grants, and — even though you don't have the resources of Bill Gates — you also have a responsibility to donate wisely. The most effective charities are those that are very focused, that have a specific goal. Don't get caught up in the charity of the moment or fall for a scam. Make sure the charity you have in mind is deserving of your donation. Before you give, investigate the charity (charitywatch.org or charitynavigator.org are two sources) and find out how much it spends on fundraising and administrative costs. The less spent on those categories, the better. That means your donation will go to the actual work of the charity.

You don't have to be a billionaire or multimillionaire to share what you have with others. According to the Vedic scriptures (and other spiritual teachings), it is a crime to have more than you need. The way to redeem yourself is to give your excess to those less fortunate than you. This results in what the modern world would call a "win-win" situation: the less fortunate person gets his needs met, and the more fortunate person relieves himself of the guilt of having too much (and all the temptations that exposes him to) and experiences the joy of being able to help someone else. Giving is getting.

The same is true for those with the second T, "talent." By talent, I don't mean singing, dancing, or other performance abilities. In this case, a talent can be anything you can do that would be helpful to someone else: an accountant who helps poor people fill out their tax forms; a knitter who makes blankets for children in the hospital; a teenager who mows the lawn for his elderly neighbor. If you have been blessed with certain useful talents, then it is a crime not to use them in service to others.

As I mentioned in the previous chapter, charitable organizations are always in need of people with different skills. If an organization asks you for a monetary donation and you can't afford to make one at the time, ask them if you can donate a service instead. The current trend of social entrepreneurship—using entrepreneurial skills to address social problems—is changing the whole landscape of charity work. Instead of simply giving away food or trucking in water to a place suffering from a drought, for example, these social entrepreneurs focus on ways to improve farming practices and infrastructure so that a drought won't have such devastating effects in the future. Social entrepreneurs believe in the Chinese proverb, "Give a man a fish and you feed him for a day. Teach a man to fish and you feed him for a lifetime."

Even if you believe you don't have any skills to share, you have the third *T*, "time." Take a few minutes to listen to your spouse when he or she is telling you about the day or to go outside and play with your young children. Go visit your neighbor with the failing eyesight and ask if he wants you to read him the newspaper or a book. Invite the new family next door over for dinner. Maybe you can't afford to pay people big checks, but you can always afford to pay attention. Don't multitask when you are spending time with someone. Look at them while they're talking. Ask questions or repeat what they've said back to them to show that you're listening and that you care.

I could add a fourth *T* — thanks. More than ever, there is importance in saying, thank you to others. We have forgotten the art of sending gracious thank-you notes. Handwritten notes can really make a difference in the lives of the writer and the recipient. Take a moment to write a thank-you note to a waitress, the coffee counter attendant, the checkout clerk, or the greeter at the front of the Walmart store. When you appreciate the small things people do for you, it broadens your mind and your heart.

The vital thing to remember is that you always have something to give. It is often what doesn't cost us any-thing — a smile, a blessing, a prayer, a handshake, a hug — that turns out to be the most valuable gift of all, especially when it is given in the proper spirit.

How you give is just as important, if not more so, than what you give. When you give wholeheartedly, with no expectation of a gift in return or even thanks for what you have done, you are the most in touch with the divinity with us all. Charity brings out the best in people. Have you ever noticed how generous little children can be? The ones I have met are always happy to share whatever treasure they have at the moment—their pet frog, a doll, or a lollipop. The saying goes that a task can be "as easy as taking candy from a baby," but in my experience, you don't need to take anything from a baby. The baby will gladly give it to you. Little children are perhaps the best examples of the way Roman Stoic philosopher Seneca advised us all to be: "We should give as we would receive, cheerfully, quickly, and without hesitation," Seneca wrote, "for there is no grace in a benefit that sticks to the fingers."

"The Gift of the Magi" is a short story by American writer O. Henry that portrays the proper spirit of giving. In it, a young married couple, very poor, love each other so much that they are willing to sacrifice their most precious possessions in order to surprise each other with the perfect gift. The husband pawns his treasured watch to buy a beautiful set of combs for his wife's hair, while the wife cuts her hair and sells it to pay for a platinum chain for her husband's watch. Some would call these young lovers foolish, but O. Henry believes differently. "[L]et it be said that of all who give gifts these two were the wisest. O all who give and receive gifts such as they are wisest. Everywhere they are wisest. They are the magi."

The reason these two were the wisest givers is that they gave without thinking of themselves but only of the other person. And while this sentiment is easily understandable in a couple very much in love, imagine how much more blessed is the one who gives so unselfishly to a total stranger, as in "The Wise Woman's Stone," an anonymous story collected in *The Best of Bits and Pieces* by Arthur Lenehan. In the tale, a wise woman traveling in the mountains found a precious stone in a stream and tucked it into her bag. The next day she met a hungry traveler and opened her bag to share her food with him. But the minute he saw the precious stone inside, he forgot all about food. He asked the wise woman to give him the stone instead. She handed it over without hesitation, and the traveler went away, knowing the stone was valuable enough to supply his needs for the rest of his life. Yet something about the exchange troubled him, and he returned to the wise woman and gave the stone back to her. "I know how valuable the stone is, but I give it back in the hope that you can give me something even more precious," he said. "Give me what you have within you that enabled you to give me the stone."

Because he acknowledges that the serenity and self-lessness of the wise woman is more valuable that any precious stone, the traveler is well on his way to experiencing the joy that enabled her to give so freely. What he will also discover is that the wise woman got more joy out of giving him the stone than he received from the gift. This is what I mean by the seeming paradox that giving is getting. "It is one of the most beautiful compensations of this life that no man can sincerely try to help another without helping himself," wrote the American transcendentalist philosopher Ralph Waldo Emerson.

That sincerity of intention is the key to experiencing the joy of giving. People who think of giving as a chore to be performed, who grudgingly give their 10 percent tithe to charity or who complain about gift-giving occasions as if they were being robbed, do not experience the joy of giving. Neither do those who give just to be noticed for their good works. Writing a few decades after Emerson, at the turn of the twentieth century, India's spiritual ambassador to America, Swami Vivekananda, explained why it is more blessed to give than to receive: "Do not stand on a high pedestal and take five cents in your hand and say, 'Here, my poor man,' but be grateful that the poor man is there, so by making a gift to him you are able to help yourself," he wrote. "It is not the receiver that is blessed, but it is the giver. Be thankful that you are allowed to exercise your power of benevolence and mercy in the world, and thus become pure and perfect."

The belief that we get more from giving is not just based on anecdotes and teachings like these, but also on sociological research. A study by Stephan Meier and Alois Stutzer asked, "Is volunteering rewarding in itself?" The answer was a resounding yes. "The results of this study support not only the notion that volunteering influences happiness but also that evidence is presented for the reverse causation: happy people are more likely to volunteer," they concluded. "Volunteering increases happiness, which in turn increases the likelihood of volunteering."

Sometimes what researchers discover when interviewing people runs counter to some well-known theories. Take psychologist Abraham Maslow and his hierarchy of needs theory, which suggests that people need to fulfill certain needs to attain happiness. Researchers from the University of Illinois who tested this theory found that it was basically true that people who had their basic needs (food, shelter, safety, and so on) met were happier on the whole. But they also discovered something that Maslow hadn't put into his equation: that higher life evaluations were also shown to be closely related to the fulfillment of *other* people's needs, not just one's own. In other words, those who helped others rated themselves happier than those who didn't.

That conclusion makes me think back to my summer wanderings with the monks when I was a child in India. In every small village, our group of monks was always greeted with such joy by people who possessed very little themselves. Looking back, I see how easy it would have been for them to look the other way, to rationalize that they barely had enough to feed and clothe themselves, much less a band of wandering monks. But they never did. They opened up their hearts and their houses to us and shared their meager supplies with us so generously. It was obvious even to me that their generosity rebounded to them with great happiness. I could tell from their smiles and laughter and the happy songs that greeted us wherever we went. Truly for these poor villagers, giving was getting.

The great truths of this life are often expressed as paradoxes. "Giving is getting" is one of those truths. And that brings me back to Sir John Templeton, renowned in the business world for dramatically increasing his own wealth and that of his clients through his shrewd investments. He may be the richest person I ever met, but undoubtedly he was also the person least affected by his wealth.

"I made many people very rich, and in that process, I also acquired enormous wealth. However, I did not realize the real value of the wealth until 1961 when I started the Templeton Prize for Science and Spirituality," he told me. "When I started giving money to various causes, I realized that the real joy of money is to give it away."

Sir John Templeton inspired me more than many sages, saints, and monks in all of my pilgrimages in India and other places. He was the embodiment of a living, walking, talking, and touching human being full of love, joy, and happiness. He never bragged about it, but it was always radiating from him. The glow of content on his face and the aura of calm and quiet around him were unparalleled. You do not run into that sort of person every day.

His guiding principle about happiness was that you should give away the things you love most. If you love money, give all of the money that you can and whatever is left will be nothing but pure joy and happiness. If you love people, give all of the love you can to all of the people in the world, and whatever is left will be nothing but pure joy and happiness.

Investors like Sir John are not content to save their money and earn a small amount of interest. Instead, they take greater risks in the hope that their reward will be greater. Sir John felt the same way about happiness, except he never thought the investment of happiness was a risk. To him, it was a sure thing. To him, giving was getting. "If we try hard to bring happiness to others, we cannot stop it from coming to us also," he said. "To get joy, we must give it, and to keep joy, we must scatter it."

Checklist:

Take a few minutes to determine where you are on the happiness scale right now, on a scale of one to ten.

Now meditate for a while on these questions:

- What talents do you have to share with others?

- How can you make the most of your charitable donations?

- What do you get when you give to others?

Reminder for today:

Today I will give what I can to others, even if it is only a word of thanks or a blessing.

8

Healthiness Is Happiness and Vice Versa

Our body is a machine for living. It is organized for that, it is its nature. Let life go on in it unhindered and let it defend itself, it will do more than if you paralyze it by encumbering it with remedies.

— LEO TOLSTOY

Even though we are spiritual beings having a human experience on this earth, that doesn't mean we should ignore the bodies that our spirits inhabit. We are not our bodies, but we do exist in them, and we have a responsibility to maintain them.

Your body is what carries your soul on this earth, just as vehicles carry our bodies from one place to another.

What if you were told when you got your car that it was the only one you could ever have, that you would have no chance to ever buy or trade for another, no replacement if it gets wrecked? More than likely, you would take very good care of it. You would check the fluid levels in the engine and the air pressure in the tires. You would keep the exterior washed and waxed and the interior clean. You would take it to a mechanic for regular maintenance and at the first hint of a problem. You would drive carefully and responsibly.

Yet too many of us don't give the same level of care to our bodies. We eat junk food and don't get regular check-ups. We let our muscles get flabby. We get too much sun and not enough sleep. We forget to brush and floss our teeth. We smoke and drink and pop pills. In other words, we treat our bodies as if we could trade them in for a new model every few years.

But we can't. We only get one body in this life. Your body is a temple that you have been given to maintain with loving care for a lifetime. How well you care for your body determines how long you will live, even a century and longer.

According to Vedic scriptures, all human beings are entitled to live a long and healthy life of at least one hundred years, divided into four separate and important stages. The first twenty-five years should be invested in learning and acquiring the skills to have a successful career. The next twenty-five years, from age twenty-six to fifty, should be devoted to raising children, so that they may be an asset for the greater society. After age fifty, the individual should start focusing more on the self-discovery process and meditating upon the real questions of existence: Who am I? Why am I here? How can I make this world better than I found it? The last twenty-five years are the years of renunciation, rejuvenation, and enlightenment.

But you will never complete these important stages if you do not take care of your body, which is why caring for your physical body is also an important spiritual responsibility. It also determines how happy you will be because you cannot enjoy a long life if you are unhealthy. We all desire to live long, but sometimes we behave as if we don't. It is ironic that advancements in our culture—like plentiful food and indoor jobs—have had unintentional negative consequences on our health.

If the body is a "machine for living," as Tolstoy says, food is its fuel. Yet too much food, especially the wrong kinds of food, can be bad for our bodies. In America, the land of plenty, the problem for most of us is that we put in too much food. We are killing ourselves slowly with fork, knife, and spoon. About 68 percent of people in the United States are either overweight or obese, the Centers for Disease Control and Prevention reported in 2010. The developing countries are not far behind. The latest reports from countries like India and China show that the fastest-growing illnesses in these newly rich nations are heart disease and type two diabetes, both of which are the result of growing prosperity and a sedentary lifestyle.

People seem to think that the answer to their weight problem will always be found in the next fad diet that comes around. They count carbs and calories. They order special meals delivered to their home. They go to meetings to weigh themselves and calculate exchanges. They keep charts and diaries. They buy nonfat and low-sugar foods. They shun red meat and dairy products. They take drugs. They skip dessert. And yet they almost always gain back the weight they lost.

Yo-yo dieting—the process of gaining pounds, losing them, and gaining them back—has helped make weight loss a $55 billion industry around the world, with Americans spending about $40 billion of that figure.

It's one of the most successful ways of capitalizing on failure that exists today. The diet industry is betting that you will fail, and (like most dieters) they seldom lose.

The same can be said of the exercise industry, which profits from good intentions that are not put into practice. One industry publication estimates that more than 80 percent of the 40 million Americans paying for gym memberships are not using them—a waste of $12 billion annually. These figures don't include money spent on at-home exercise equipment, workout videos, gym shoes, and clothes that gather dust from disuse.

Like the path to happiness, the way to true health and fitness is simple but not easy: eat less and move more. What makes it successful is that it is the only weight loss and fitness plan that is sustainable over your whole life. And the key to making it sustainable is incorporating it into your daily routine in a way that is enjoyable, that doesn't make it seem like you are sacrificing pleasure or doing chores.

Let's look at diet first. There's no joy in giving up foods that you love because they contain too much sugar or too much fat. It's not even practical to deprive yourself completely because, as any failed dieter will tell you, abstinence only sharpens your cravings for forbidden foods. Substituting nonfat or sugar-free foods for the real things also doesn't work because they don't satisfy your appetite and leave you feeling empty. These are the reasons diets fail.

So what's the solution? "Moderation. Small helpings. Sample a little bit of everything," according to Julia Child, author of *Mastering the Art of French Cooking* and perhaps America's best-known TV cook. "These are the secrets of happiness and good health." We can trust what she says because, despite her love of butter and cream, she lived just a few days short of ninety-two years.

Choose what you eat for taste and health, opting for organic and natural foods whenever possible to avoid the extras you don't need in most packaged and processed products. Filling your body with junk and fast food doesn't give it the fuel it needs, and a diet like this will leave you feeling tired and ill. As the computer programmers say, "Garbage in, garbage out." Your body is a temple; do not fill it with garbage.

Food is also medicine and often the best source of nutrients because the body can process them more efficiently in food than in vitamins and supplements. Eat a variety of foods, a balanced diet, to ensure you get the nutrients you need.

You should also drink plenty of water each day — about eight glasses or more. Your body is about 70 percent water and needs to be replenished and refreshed for you to feel your best. If you drink water with your meal or just before, you feel full faster and are less likely to overeat.

Listen to your body. Eat when you are hungry and stop when you are full. Enjoy what you eat; take the time to savor each bite. That way you will leave the table more satisfied than if you had mindlessly shoveled in your meal.

Your daily exercise should also be something you enjoy. Otherwise, you won't make it a habit. Think about an activity that brings you joy or a skill you've always wanted to learn and make that the way you exercise. If you like Latin music, you could take a salsa dance class. If you like being alone in nature, you could take a daily walk on a trail. You can also incorporate more movement into your everyday activities by taking the stairs instead of the elevator, parking farther away from buildings, and walking instead of driving short distances.

Even as you strive to improve your body, do it with an attitude of love. Love your body, no matter its size or shape. Most serial dieters and gym dropouts have failed because—instead of making healthiness their goal—they are trying to remake their bodies in the form of some unachievable ideal—a super-thin supermodel or a muscle-bound movie star. Take a good, positive look at your body. The human body is an amazing work of art and a fascinating, complex creation. Admire your body for what it is, right at this moment. Accept it and love it. Don't compare your body to anyone else's. Don't criticize any of your features or wish for something different.

Instead, take an inventory of your body and appreciate what is good about the way you look, the way you feel, and the way your body performs for you. Your senses alone make every day a pleasure, allowing you to hear the birds sing, see the sunset, feel the breeze blowing across your skin, taste a peach, and smell fresh-cut grass. Your heart beats about seventy-two times a minute, circulating your blood throughout your body. Your lungs fill with air and supply oxygen to your blood. Your feet take you where you want to go. Your hands reach for what you want to hold. And all this happens with very little thought on your part.

Is there any man-made machine that is this reliable, this intuitive, and this easy to maintain? All it needs is food, water, exercise, and rest to keep running for a lifetime. The needs of the body are simple, and we should let that simplicity guide our lives in general. "Life is really simple, but we insist on making it complicated," said the Chinese philosopher Confucius.

In general, if you take good care of your body, it will take good care of you. However, sometimes illness, disease, or an accident happens, and your body suffers. I was reminded of that fact in just the past year, when I went to the hospital for the first time in my life, with pneumonia in both lungs. The good news was that because of my healthy lifestyle, positive attitude, and personal attention from caring physicians, I was able to recover from the illness much more quickly than most people my age.

Unfortunately, though, modern medicine too often treats only the body and not the person, only the symptoms and not the causes. Personal attention from physicians is seen as less important than the latest technical advances or pharmaceutical discoveries.

"Medicine is spiritually ill," according to Dr. Allan Hamilton, acclaimed neurosurgeon and author of *The Scalpel and the Soul*. The doctor admits that he was robot-like in his attendance on his own patients, until he became a patient himself. As a result of a serious back injury during Operation Desert Storm, he found himself lying flat on his back in a full-body cast with plenty of time to ponder ways to use computer image-guided techniques to treat tumors in the body. He also observed how little time the team of orthopedic surgeons working on his case actually spent talking with him.

Dr. Hamilton says that we spend fifteen to twenty minutes to decide on a hotel or resort and fifty minutes picking which car to buy. But an average surgeon spends less than seven minutes with a patient before surgery. The way medicine is practiced in our country has really made it so mechanized that the human element is almost overlooked. "Less than seven minutes with the surgeon is not enough to know the patient," he said.

Dr. Hamilton went on to become a powerful advocate for bridging the gap between medicine and spirituality. "There is more to medicine than surgery and prescriptions. Faith, hope, and spirituality are all part of healing and recovery," he says.

While Dr. Hamilton and others in the medical profession encourage their colleagues to take more time talking to their patients, other advocates are pushing patients to become more involved and active in their own treatment instead of relying passively on a doctor's advice. Both movements show the important role mind and spirituality play in the healing of the body.

Dave deBronkart, author of *Laugh, Sing and Eat Like a Pig*, is one of those activists. When he was diagnosed with kidney cancer that had already spread throughout his body, deBronkart decided to do all he could to help himself heal. He was inspired by the remarkable recovery of *Saturday Evening Post* editor Norman Cousins, who largely credited laughing at Marx Brothers movies for his comeback from a disease that was supposed to be incurable in his book *Anatomy of an Illness*. As the title of his own book indicates, deBronkart's strategy focused on doing things that gave him pleasure and lifted his spirits, like enjoying comedy, singing in his barbershop quartet group, and eating high-calorie foods. Best of all, he was supported in all this by his physician, his family, and his friends. And he did recover.

By laughing in the face of illness, Dave deBronkart proved to be brave and unusual. It is hard to be happy when you are ill. You are more than your body, but that body has a powerful influence on your mood. Yet the reverse is also true — that a positive attitude leads to longer life and to surprising recoveries from serious illness — like Dave deBronkart's.

Perhaps you are reading this book because you feel happiness has gone out of your life due to serious or chronic illness, the aches and pains of aging, or a general feeling of depression. "If only I were healthier, I'd feel happier," you may think. To a certain extent, the opposite is true as well: If you were happier, you would feel healthier. The mind has a powerful effect on the body. The Vedic sage Vasistha attributes the cause of many diseases to disturbances of the mind, what modern medicine calls psychosomatic illnesses. In the Yoga Vasistha, the sage said that when the mind is disturbed, the breath is affected, which in turn decreases the body's immune system and makes it more susceptible to disease. His cure was a regimen of yoga, meditation, and breathing exercises.

In fact, practices like these and all the others we have talked about so far as ways for you to experience happiness will also lead to healthiness. Silence, meditation, a simpler lifestyle, fulfilling work, generosity, compassion — all these practices reduce the stress in your life. And reducing stress improves health.

In the publication "Stress and Your Health," the U.S. Department of Health and Human Services confirms that stress hormones increase blood pressure, heart rate and blood sugar levels, and that long-term stress contributes to depression, anxiety, obesity, heart disease, high blood pressure, abnormal heartbeat, menstrual problems, and acne.

Wouldn't it be nice to be able to use something natural and noninvasive to relieve stress and to treat these other conditions? As it is, America is a nation of pill-poppers, with prescription drug use rising each year, according to the Centers for Disease Control and Prevention. In a 2010 report, "U.S. Prescription Drug Data for 2007–2008," the center reported that 48 percent of Americans — nearly half the nation — took at least one prescription drug in the past month. Nine out of ten older Americans used a drug that often, and even one out of five children took a prescription drug the previous month.

Granted, sometimes prescription drugs are necessary to treat certain problems. My doctor has prescribed certain drugs for me. But it seems to me that drugs should be the last resort when it comes to treating most illnesses, not the first solution that comes to mind. For example, look at the number of schoolchildren who are taking medication for attention deficit disorder: about 2.5 million, according to the Centers for Disease Control. First of all, I wonder how many of those children have been correctly diagnosed or if some of them just need better discipline to control themselves in the classroom. Even if correctly diagnosed, do that many children need to be medicated, or would they fare just as well by getting more exercise, eating a healthier diet, and spending less time on the computer and watching television?

Likewise, among the most commonly prescribed drugs for teens and young and middle-aged adults were antidepressants. Do that many people need a chemical to lift their mood or are there other ways to combat depression without relying on a pill?

There is one form of medication with no negative side effects and impressive results: laughter. You've heard it said that laughter is the best medicine, and now research has shown that laughter can be beneficial to your health. Various studies have concluded that laughter can improve blood flow, immune response, blood sugar levels, and sleep patterns. And even though some physicians remain skeptical about the healing power of laughter, nearly all agree that it does no harm.

Even fake laughter, as practiced in six thousand Social Laughter Clubs in about sixty countries inspired by Dr. Madan Kataria of Mumbai, India, has been shown to improve immunity and decrease illness among its practitioners. Laughter yoga combines unconditional laughter with yogic breathing (Pranayama) in a class or other social setting. At first the laughter is simulated as a body exercise in a group, but soon it becomes the contagious real thing. Whether it's fake or real, the laughter has the same physiological and psychological benefits on the body. And they're all good. Try to have at least one hearty laugh each day, even if you have to fake it.

Staying healthy, like feeling happy, is simple but not easy. The only weight loss and fitness plan that consistently works is to eat less and move more. It's the only plan that is sustainable over your whole life. And the key to making it sustainable is incorporating it into your daily routine in a way that is enjoyable, that doesn't make it seem like you are sacrificing pleasure or doing chores. So make sure to develop a healthiness habit along with your happiness habit.

Checklist:

Take a few minutes to determine where you are on the happiness scale right now, on a scale of one to ten.

Now meditate for a while on these questions:

- What healthy foods can you incorporate into your daily diet?

- What activities can you do each day that will make exercising fun?

- How do you feel after a good laugh?

Reminder for today:

Today I treated my body as a temple.

9

The Habit of Happiness

If I ever go looking for my heart's desire again, I won't look any further than my own back yard. Because if it isn't there, I never really lost it to begin with! Is that right?

— DOROTHY IN *"THE WIZARD OF OZ"*

When you first picked up this book, more than likely it was because you weren't feeling very happy. You were searching for that feeling of contentment, inner peace, satisfaction, bliss, and joy that was missing from your life. You had experienced happiness before, so you knew how good it felt, but then you lost it. Or did you?

Let's think for a while about what it means when something is "lost." It's true that in some cases, an item can be lost to us forever—letters or photographs burned in a house fire or a piece of jewelry stolen by a thief and melted down for its gold. But usually when we speak of a thing as being "lost," it means that we can't find it. We have misplaced it or forgotten where we put it. Unless it has sprouted legs and run away, the item is exactly in the same place it was the last time we had it—if only we could remember where that was!

Even sometimes when we realize that our happiness is within us and we know where we should go and what we should do to find it again, we can become so distracted by the outside world that we look for happiness in all the wrong places. Have you heard the old joke about the man who lost a precious coin? He was searching high and low for the coin in the marketplace and all his friends and neighbors came over to help. Finally one asked where the man had been when he lost the coin.

"In my basement," he said.

"In your basement!" the friend cried. "Then why on earth are you looking for the coin out here?"

"Because the light's better out here," he replied.

The same is true for happiness. I hope I have convinced you by now that happiness is not out there somewhere for you to chase after. Happiness is within you; it always has been. Happiness is you. So you haven't lost happiness. You just need to remember where you can find it.

This sounds easy, but it isn't. It requires some work on your part and a certain level of self-awareness. It requires you to think, to speak, and to act on all the principles discussed in this book. That's why each chapter ends with a list of questions and a recommendation for action. Review, repetition, and response are all ways to improve your memory. When you remember to be happy, you will be happy.

That is why I have emphasized the importance of cultivating the habit of happiness. A habit is a behavior that you perform so often that you no longer think about it; after a while it just comes to you naturally. A good habit, like remembering to be happy, can be woven into the fabric of your everyday life, keeping you in a stable, secure state of mind.

By the same token, bad habits are hard to break. Much of this book has been devoted to encouraging you to unlearn some of the habits of today's modern life. This unlearning is probably the most difficult part of the process. You will be swimming against the tide when you start to disconnect yourself from the Internet, silence your phone, and turn off your television. After being so connected and so busy 24/7, you will find it hard to adjust to even five or ten minutes of complete silence at first. But with concentrated effort and gradual increases in your silent time, you will grow more comfortable. Nowhere is it more important than in this journey to remember that slow and steady wins the race.

You will also be unlearning desire, especially for material things. This curbing of desire and the decrease of your emphasis on obtaining worldly possessions will also run counter to mainstream American culture. Our economy may be built on consumer demand for new goods and services, but that doesn't mean that you need to go into debt by buying items that you don't need. The hedonic wheel will continue to spin even after you jump off it.

More importantly, you will replace the clamor of connection and the clutter of desires with rich, life-affirming experiences. As you silence the noise around you, you will become more attentive to your inner voice. You will become more self-aware. Your priorities will realign in the proper order. Instead of working around the clock so you can keep up with the Joneses, you will take time to ask yourself those important questions: Who am I? Why am I here? What am I doing with my life? What makes me feel truly happy? And you will begin to find the answers to those questions.

What's important to remember is that this kind of self-discovery is not a quick, one-shot process. Just as you can't go on a fad diet for a week and expect to lose twenty pounds or use a treadmill for thirty minutes on the weekend and expect to run a marathon, you have to work on your happiness habit. It's not a part-time or weekend-only activity. You need to practice it every day. You have to talk the talk and walk the walk. Incorporate happiness into your life the same way you do other good habits, like washing your hands and brushing your teeth.

In fact, that might be a good place to begin making happiness a habit—by pairing a reminder to be happy with your already established habits. For example, you might use the time you are brushing your teeth to meditate on one of the day's questions. You might imagine yourself washing away all your desires and mental clutter as you wash your hands before eating.

People form habits in different ways, so no one method works well for everyone. I have begun with a simple checklist as a reminder, but you may customize your own way for making happiness a habit in your personal life. Here are some other suggestions:

A happiness buddy. I mentioned the idea of a happiness buddy in reference to your work, but a buddy could be your spouse, a member of your family, or a friend instead of a co-worker. Ideally, your happiness buddy will have read this book too, and you will both be willing to help each other incorporate its principles into your lives. Over a meal or at some other convenient time, share some of the thoughts you had during your meditation period and compare ideas about how to put your thoughts into action. Check in on each other and give each other encouragement. While other people can't make you happy, they can support and affirm the happiness within you.

A happiness club. This is an expanded version of the happiness buddy. One way to build a habit is to stick to a schedule, so if you and other happiness buddies come together once or twice a week for an organized activity, you will help each other build a happiness habit. Your activity could vary, but it should be something supportive of happiness. For example, perhaps your group comes together to practice yoga or even laughing meditation. You may function more like a traditional support group, in which you report on your progress for the week and ask for advice for improvement. Perhaps your group takes on a public service or charitable project to help others. Whatever form or purpose it takes, just remember that the group is there to support individual happiness. Don't let it become one of those calendar-cluttering commitments that is more of a drain than an inspiration.

A happy place. "Finding your happy place" has become a cliché for escaping from day-to-day reality. But going to a special location—whether physically or mentally—can be a way to reduce stress and gain a new perspective. For some, it may be in a sunny garden surrounded by flowers and birds, while for others it may be the cozy corner of a dark library with the musty smell of old books. If you can't get away to the actual physical location, close your eyes and imagine yourself there for a few minutes, while you are on hold for a phone call or when you are riding the bus. A mental vacation can be as refreshing as an actual one.

A happy time. We each have a favorite time of day. For some, the rising sun makes dawn a time of hope and promise, while others feel satisfaction and contentment in the evening when the sun sets. For schoolchildren, it's the time when the bell rings and freedom begins. For lovers, it's the stillness of a moonlit night. One person I know says the best time of day is the time just before the dawn, when you can better bear the darkness because you know the light is on its way. Whatever your favorite time of day, use it to reflect on happiness.

A happy song. A time-honored way to teach new concepts is through song. How many of you learned the alphabet that way? The right song can get the day off to a good start or lift your mood when you need it most. What song makes you feel happy?

Happy thoughts. There's a saying that to fall asleep, count your blessings instead of sheep. When we take a few moments to remember the happy moments of our lives and the happy faces of those we love, we feel warmth and contentment growing inside us. Sure, it can help us get to sleep, but it can also help us when we face a difficult time in life to remember what it feels like to be happy.

Happy pictures. Once when I went to get my blood drawn at the hospital, I noticed that the nurse had covered her cubicle with photos of polar bears. When I asked if she liked polar bears, she replied with a big smile, "Doesn't everyone?" Obviously, pictures of polar bears made her happy and she thought they would also happily distract her patients when they were getting stuck by a needle. Images are powerful mood influencers. If you are surrounded all day by sad or stressed faces or scenes of unrest and destruction on television, these images will affect your mood. Make sure to have some photos of happy faces and places in spots where they will catch your eye — as a background on your computer, on your walls, on your bookshelf, in your wallet.

Happiness reminders, low tech and high tech. When Stephen Covey's *Seven Habits of Highly Successful People* became such a huge bestseller, his company and others capitalized on products and services beyond the book to help readers incorporate the habits into their daily lives. Soon seminars, webinars, audiotapes, videotapes, posters, calendars, journals, and software reminders of the "Seven Habits" were everywhere. I don't know what kind of reminder works best for you. Perhaps it's as simple as a sticky note on your computer or a piece of paper stuck to the refrigerator with a magnet. Or maybe it's an electronic reminder that pops up on your iPad at a certain time of day, perhaps with an accompanying beep. Some people send themselves e-mail reminders, then click on the reminder to add to their task bar for the day. And I'm sure there are still a few people who tie a bit of string around their finger. What's important is to use what works for you.

Happiness journal. It has been proven that we remember something better if we write it down. The physical act of writing enhances our memory of the words we form. So you may want to record your happiness journey with diary or journal entries. What are the thoughts that came to you during your meditation? What actions did you resolve to do? What happened when you acted? How are you decreasing your mental clutter? How are you curbing desires? What are you discovering about yourself and others as you do? Writing down your thoughts and then reviewing them later will remind you of the important principles you became aware of along your journey and keep you on the right path.

Even though happiness is you, it makes sense to speak of the discovery of happiness as a journey, a journey within. Just as Dorothy needed to take a long trip down the Yellow Brick Road, conquer a wicked witch, and face down the wizard before she realized where her true happiness lay, we have much to learn about ourselves on our happiness journey.

The work of this self-discovery is a joy in itself, as we begin to tune out the noisy interference of the outside world. The more we meditate on happiness, the more we realize that the external world has no notion of what brings true happiness. Instead, the material world tempts us with desires and pleasures that appeal to our external senses. The material world pushes us onto the hedonic wheel, where we run without ceasing, chasing after desires and pleasures but never getting any closer to happiness.

As we meditate, we tune in to the divinity within us. That divinity helps us recognize the divinity within others and teaches us to treat them with empathy and compassion. Increasing the happiness of others increases our own. Suddenly we begin to see the world differently. Work is not just a paycheck that allows us to buy more material goods than our neighbors. Work is worship, a way to act out our beliefs and principles. A panhandler who asks us for money is no longer a beggar; he is an opportunity for us to practice our generosity, sometimes with money and sometimes with a prayer or a smile.

The more time we spend in meditation, practicing yoga, taking quiet walks, and eating simple, nutritious food, the better we feel both spiritually and physically. Our stress level goes down as we become less concerned with acquiring things and as we turn down the volume and the pressures of our lives. We concern ourselves with important matters and what is unimportant either takes care of itself or goes away. We spend more time with the ones we love. We give them our time and our attention. We listen to what they say. We treat friend and stranger alike the way we want to be treated. We live our lives differently than we did before. We are happy.

The people we encounter in our lives notice we are different. When you are happy, that happiness emanates from within you. Others feel your good vibrations. Your happiness is contagious. You can pass it on generously to anyone you come in contact with. Best of all, this sharing of happiness does not diminish your own happiness in any way. In fact, it makes it grow.

And do we live happily ever after? We definitely can, although not in that fairytale way. Instead of thinking of "ever after," we need to live fully in the moment we have now, without fretting or holding grudges about what has happened in the past or worrying about what may happen in the future.

This is not to say that nothing bad will ever happen to us. We all are subject to the same calamities in this world: death, disease, and destruction are as likely to strike a happy person as one who is unhappy. How we respond to hardship is where you see the difference. The unhappy person will see these external factors as the cause of his misery and will grow helpless and sad as he continues to blame the world for his troubles. The happy person may experience a short time of disappointment or grief, but he will bounce back because he knows these troubles are temporary and outside of him. Inside, he is still the same. He is still happy.

The importance of our response is illustrated in the story of a samurai warrior who encountered a monk on his way back from battle. "Oh, monk," the samurai began humbly, "which is the way to heaven and which is the way to hell?" The monk, who was deep in meditation, did not answer. The samurai asked again, louder, and a third time, louder still. His yelling shook the tree sheltering the monk.

The monk's eyes flew open. "You stupid fellow! Why did you disturb my meditation?"

The samurai was furious. Who was this monk to call him stupid? He drew his sword, ready to kill the monk.

When he did, the monk just smiled and said, "That is the way to hell."

The warrior stopped where he stood, realizing that the monk had been listening to him all along and was now teaching him a valuable lesson. He put his sword back in its sheath.

"And that is the way to heaven," the monk told him.

The happy person is like a lifetime farmer. In some years, the rains come, the sun shines, and the harvests are good. But in other years, there may be droughts or floods, disease or insects that destroy the crop. Yet, good year or bad year, the farmer remains. His identity is as a farmer and no ill that comes to his farm will change that. He doesn't blame himself when crops are bad or boast about himself when crops are good. He just makes the best of what comes his way and perseveres as a farmer because that's who he is.

The way Swami Dayananda explains the difference is through the words used to express happiness (sukham) and sorrow (duhkam) compared to "I am happy" (sukhi) and "I am sad" (duhkhi). While good-intentioned people often rush in to try to help with the sorrow, the external factor, the real problem is in the person's attitude, that he is sorrowful.

Here's how poet John Milton described the difference in attitude:

He that has light within his own clear breast
May sit in the centre, and enjoy bright day:
But he that hides a dark soul and foul thoughts
Benighted walks under the mid-day sun;
Himself his own dungeon.

This is another way of saying, "The problem is you. The solution is you."

I leave you with a story about the power of attitude. It is the story of the contest between the Sun and the North

Wind to see who was the greater power. After much boasting on both sides, they finally agreed that whichever of the two who could remove the coat of the next man walking down the road would indeed be the greater. The North Wind went first and blew a terrible, cold gale. But instead of having his coat blown off, the man held onto it all the tighter to stay warm. The North Wind finally gave up, and the Sun came out beautiful and warm for his turn. The kind warmth of his rays finally made the man loosen up his coat and take it off as he walked. As usual, the sunnier disposition won the day.

You can have that same sunny disposition in your life. Now that you have become aware of some of the ways to simplify your lifestyle, develop compassion, curb your desires, give of yourself, and other aspects of happy living that you can incorporate into your daily life, it is up to you to make happiness a habit. If you can do that, this is the last happiness book you'll have to buy!

Checklist:

Take a few minutes to determine where you are on the happiness scale right now, on a scale of one to ten.

Now meditate for a while on these questions:

- How can I incorporate happiness into my daily routines?

- What reminders can I use to keep on the right path?

- How do I respond to disappointments in life?

Reminder for today:

Today I will live in the moment and enjoy every moment of my life.

1 0

Happiness Checklist

1. Today I spent time alone without feeling lonely.

2. Today I paid attention to the little things in life that make me happy.

3. Today I meditated and attained a tranquil mind.

4. Today I conquered the enemies of happiness — desires, anger, delusion, greed, guilt, attachment, deception, jealousy, and most of all, ego.

5. Today I didn't judge anyone by his appearance and treated everyone as I wanted to be treated.

6. Today I had a positive attitude toward work and in all my dealings with other people.

7. Today I gave what I could to others, even if it was only a word of thanks or a blessing.

8. Today I treated my body as a temple.

9. Today I lived in the moment and enjoyed every moment of my life.

Appendix: More on Meditation and Yoga

First of all, I want to clarify that *yoga* is not a word used in ancient scriptures. Instead, the Vedic scriptures referred to *yog*. But the word *yoga*, as it was first called in America, has spread around the world. Now even people in India often say *yoga* rather than *yog*, so I will too.

Yoga was first written about nearly two thousand years ago by the sage Patangali, author of *"Yog-darshan."* The sage meditated and found out that the real purpose of yoga is to attain the Almighty God or what I refer to in the book as the divinity within us all.

Many books and manuals have tried to translate the verses from this pioneering book. The most famous interpreter of yoga in America was a thirty-year-old Indian monk named Swami Vivekananda. On September 11, 1893, Swami Vivekananda addressed the opening of the August Parliament of Religion in Chicago and held the four thousand attendees spellbound with a series of show-stopping improvised talks, according to "How Yoga Won the West," an article in the July 10, 2011, *New York Times* Sunday Review by Ann Louise Bardach, who is writing a biography of Vivekananda. Vivekananda simplified the whole Vedanta (the knowledge portion of the Vedic scriptures) into a few teachings that were accessible and irresistible to Westerners, Ms. Bardach writes. He was very effective in explaining key ideas, such as how "all souls are potentially divine" and how work is worship.

"By the end of his last Chicago lecture on September 27, Vivekananda was a star. And like the enterprising Americans he so admired, he went on the road to pitch his message, thus dazzling some of the great minds of his time," Ms. Bardach writes. During his tour of America, he spread the basic teachings of Vedanta, mesmerizing his close followers and other attendees with his marathon meditation sessions.

Today yoga has become a vast, six-billion-dollar industry in America, with millions of people from all walks of life doing strenuous physical exercise regularly in the name of yoga.

But yoga is more than an exercise technique. Yogic exercises are helpful tools in attaining happiness. According to sage Patangali, if we are really interested in achieving peace, tranquility of mind, and everlasting happiness, then we have to follow Ashtang, or eight-step, yoga.

These are the eight steps as described by Swami Vivekananda:

1. **Yama** (guidelines for how to treat others). This is the most important and has to govern the whole life; it has five divisions:

   - Not injuring any being by thought, word, or deed.

   - Non-covetousness in thought, word, or deed.

   - Perfect chastity in thought, word, or deed.

   - Perfect truthfulness in thought, word, or deed.

   - Non-receiving of gifts.

2. **Niyama** (guidelines for treating yourself). The bodily care, bathing daily, dietary, etc.

3. **Asana** (posture). Hips, shoulders, and head must be held straight, leaving the spine free.

4. **Pranayama** (breathing). Restraining the breath in order to get control of the Prana or vital force.

5. **Pratyahara** (looking within). Turning the mind inward and restraining it from going outward, revolving the matter in the mind in order to understand it.

6. **Dharana** (focus). Concentrating on one subject.

7. **Dhyana** (meditation). Merging effortlessly with what you are concentrating on.

8. **Samadhi** (self-awareness). Achieving illumination, the aim of all our efforts.

You will notice that the step right before the achievement to enlightenment is meditation, which I also want to explain more in this appendix. Here is one of Swami Vivekananda's simplified descriptions of the concept:

Meditation is the gate that opens that [infinite joy] to us. Prayers, ceremonials and all the other forms of worship are simply kindergartens of meditation. You pray, you offer something.

A certain theory existed that everything raised one's spiritual power. The use of certain words, flowers, images, temples, ceremonials like the waving of lights brings the mind to that attitude, but that attitude is always in the human soul, nowhere else. People are all doing it. But what they do without knowing it, do knowingly. That is the power of meditation.

The main instrument of meditation is the mind. In trying to describe the mind to his followers, Swami Vivekananda compares it to a body of water:

The mind is like a lake, and every stone that drops into it raises waves. The waves do not let us see what we are. The full moon is reflected in the water of the lake, but the surface is so disturbed that we do not see the reflection clearly. Let it be calm. Do not let nature raise the waves. Keep quiet, and then after a little while she will give you up. Then we know what we are. God is there already, but the mind is so agitated, always running after the senses. You close the senses and yet you whirl and whirl about. Just this moment I think I am all right and I will meditate upon God, and then my mind goes to London in one minute. And if I pull it away from there, it goes to New York to think about the things I have done there in the past. These waves are to be stopped by the power of mediation.

All practitioners of meditation faced serious challenges of controlling and directing the mind. In this passage, Swami Vivekananda compares the mind to a monkey maddened by wine, a scorpion's sting, and a demon: "The human mind is like that monkey, incessantly active by its own nature; then it becomes drunk with the wine of desire, thus increasing its turbulence. After desire takes possession comes the sting of the scorpion of jealousy at the success of others, and last of all the demon of pride enters the mind, making it think itself of all importance. How hard to control such a mind!"

One way for beginners to gain control of the stubborn mind is to focus on some sights and sounds. Swami

Vivekananda has given us two nice images. In the first example, he suggests that you "imagine a lotus upon the top of the head, several inches up, with virtue as its centre, and knowledge as its stalk. The eight petals of the lotus are the eight powers of the Yogi. Inside the stamens and pistils is renunciation. If the Yogi refuses the external powers, he will come to salvation. So the eight petals of the lotus are the eight powers, but the internal stamens and pistils are extreme renunciation, the renunciation of all these powers. Inside of that lotus, think of the Golden One, the Almighty, the Intangible, He whose name is Om, the Inexpressible, surrounded with effulgent light. Meditate on that."

In a second example, he suggests that you "think of a space in your heart, and in the midst of that space think that a flame is burning. Think of that flame as your own soul and inside the flame is another effulgent light, and that is the Soul of your soul, God. Meditate on that in your heart."

Now, as I've emphasized throughout the book, this will be a gradual process. You won't be able to achieve all eight steps overnight. But if you practice the steps in order over time, then you are bound to achieve permanent peace and everlasting happiness. The only investment you have to make is your time, energy, and lots of patience. If you can find a good teacher of eight-step yoga in your area, that would be a great way to practice. Otherwise, there are plenty of audio-video programs and self-service websites that can help you to complete the arduous yet rewarding journey of eight steps.

www.ingramcontent.com/pod-product-compliance
Lightning Source LLC
Chambersburg PA
CBHW061745020426
42331CB00006B/1367

* 9 7 8 0 6 1 5 6 3 3 4 3 5 *